VERMONT
A Cultural Patchwork

Elise A. Guyette

Cobblestone Publishing, Inc.

Copy-edited by Barbara Jatkola

Designed by Outside Designs

Production and Illustrations by C. Porter Designs

Typesetting by debset

Printing and Binding by Excelsior Printing Company

Manufactured in the United States of America

ISBN 0-9607638-5-6

Cobblestone Publishing, Inc.
20 Grove Street
Peterborough, NH 03458

Cover courtesy of Shelburne Museum, Shelburne, Vermont.
Portions of the same quilt also used in section and unit openings.

Contents

Acknowledgments

The most important person I have to thank for the production of this book is my husband, David Shiman. He read every word more than once and provided valuable criticism and encouragement when needed. He unselfishly put aside his own writing to do this. For his care, patience, and untiring help with my work, I dedicate this book to him.

Other people deserve thanks as well. The most difficult section to write was the Abenaki section, since I was writing about a race different from my own. For their help with this unit, I thank John Lawyer, John Moody, Ken Maskell, and the people at the Abenaki Self Help Association in Swanton, Vermont.

Several people read parts of the book and provided me with valuable suggestions. I thank Patricia H. Kervick, Cornelia Denker, James Fitzgerald, Nilah Cote, Helen Freismuth, Marshall True, William Doyle, Faith L. Pepe, and Alice Bassett for their contributions. Thanks also to James Leddy for our discussions on ethnic Vermont.

Special thanks go to those who waded through the whole book and provided much-needed comments and criticisms. Joe Greenwald, formerly of the Shelburne Museum, was the first to read and react to an early version of this book. He allowed me to do research at the museum, where the idea for the book first sprouted. Thanks also to John Duffy and T.D. Seymour Bassett for the time they took to read the final draft. Their criticisms have made for a much better book.

Thanks also to the staffs at the Vermont Historical Society, the University of Vermont (UVM) Special Collections, the UVM Center for Rural Studies, and the UVM Center for World Education.

And finally, love to my daughter, Kathleen, who waited until I had finished the manuscript to enter the world.

Introduction

Our Patchwork

Try to imagine a patchwork quilt. Do you have one in mind? What colors catch your eye? How many different shapes and fabrics are sewn together? Imagine how much time it took to cut the materials, sew the pieces together, and quilt the layers. Many hands may have worked together designing and finishing this artistic creation. Imagine how many weeks and months were spent working on this piece of art.

As the quilt ages, changes take place. Over time, some pieces may wear out and need to be replaced. The seams may fall apart from time to time and need to be repaired. Mending does not, however, make the quilt less useful or beautiful.

Now let's reflect on the title of the book, *Vermont: A Cultural Patchwork*. Our state is comparable to a quilt. Our valleys, bodies of water, and mountains provide different colors and shapes as a backdrop for Vermont's historical patterns. People from different races and ethnic backgrounds add color and richness to our history. The hopes and dreams of thousands of people from different times and places are sewn into the fabric of our state. It took a great deal of time and effort to piece these parts together.

Note

"Ethnic" describes a group of people with common customs, history, and language.

Some people who moved to our state became permanent residents; their descendants are still here today. Some newcomers, however, found that their enthusiasm for Vermont wore thin with time, and they moved on, to be replaced by other newcomers. Sometimes things seemed to fall apart when people of different ideas clashed or one way of living was replaced by another. But Vermonters always patched up the seams and felt stronger for it.

As we piece together the history of Vermont through the readings and activities in this book, we will examine the changing patchwork of Vermont. We will find out how Vermont's mountains and valleys came to be. We will meet the people who built our state, beginning with the Abenaki, Vermont's first inhabitants. Throughout the years that followed, we will meet other groups who added to our cultural patchwork, including the French, English, Irish, and Italians. We will examine the good times and the bad times as people learned to live together and adjust to the sometimes harsh climate. We will see our state government grow and our ways of making a living change over the years. We will watch as the inhabitants scarred the land by mistreating the environment and later tried to repair the damage. We will struggle together as people of the twentieth century trying to make decisions about modern-day repairs on our old quilt. Adding new pieces and repairing the seams never ends; change never stops.

Note

Culture is the common set of customs and language shared by a group of people.

Our Culture

As the colors of our past unfold before you, you will meet people whose cultural backgrounds are different from yours. Sometimes when we encounter people with different customs, we consider the differences strange and the people alien. As you read and participate in the activities, however, we hope you will begin to recognize these differences as a beautiful part of our state. All the cultures sewn into our history add beautiful colors and shapes to our heritage. Imagine how dull a quilt would be with only one color and shape!

Note
An anthropologist is a scientist who studies cultures.

You will discover that you have many things in common with the people of the past, as well as people from different places. These things that all people have in common are called universals of culture. Anthropologists have made long lists of these universals. Here is a shortened list:

1. Languages with which to communicate.
2. Education to pass on knowledge and customs.
3. Material things to use as tools, decorations, food, etc.
4. Governments to make and enforce society's rules.
5. Conflicts and ways of resolving them.
6. Economies, which are the ways people obtain needed goods and make a living.
7. Families to love and protect each other.
8. Recreation for fun and relaxation.
9. Shelter for families and businesses.
10. Religion, which explains the spiritual workings of our world.

You will discover that all cultures share these universals, but they look different in different times and places. For instance, let's look at families, which come in all different sizes. Some are composed of the mother, father, and children, while some are single-parent families. Others may have aunts, uncles, and grandparents living with them. In some cultures, many families may live together in the same house. You will find many different customs concerning families and other universals of culture throughout the pages of this book.

Our History

This book focuses on two different approaches to history. Many history books concentrate on only famous men and women and major events. They say that these people and events are the most important aspects of our history and have made us what we are today.

Other historians believe that nameless people and everyday events have an equal claim to historical importance. This approach is known as folk history. Everyone takes part in it—you, your classmates, and your family. Each of you adds your own colors to our historical patchwork. Someday, future students will be studying the history of your way of living.

You can see from these two approaches to history that we are influenced by historical events and also influence the events of our time. This book weaves both approaches into its pages. You will read about famous people (such as Ethan Allen) and big events (such as the Great Flood of 1927), but history is more than a few individuals and great events. For that reason, this book also focuses on people whose names are long forgotten and on their everyday lives, which contributed so much to our cultural patchwork.

Student Historians

Through the activities in this book, you will be doing what historians do: reading, observing, asking questions, solving problems, thinking critically, and judging events. You will be using and sharpening many different thinking skills. To help you do this, there is a list of twenty reasoning skills in Appendix A. The numbers of these skills appear after questions and activities both in this book and ones your teacher will give you. Those numbers show you which skills you are practicing.

The easiest questions are numbered 1. The answers to those questions usually will be facts that you can copy from the text. Just finding answers on a page is not enough, however. You also must come up with some of your own answers using historical clues. As the numbers get higher, the questions will require more of your brain power to search for and find the answers.

Conducting your own investigations, creating your own answers, and making your own decisions about events is the work of real historians. It is difficult, fun, and satisfying work. Do not be afraid to come up with different answers than other historians in your class—it happens all the time among people in the history profession. As a matter of fact, it is part of the fun!

We hope you enjoy the readings and activities in this book. If you have any questions, comments, disagreements, or suggestions, feel free to write to the author c/o Cobblestone Publishing, 20 Grove Street, Peterborough, New Hampshire 03458.

SECTION I

The Making of Vermont

UNIT 1

The First People: Native Americans

Preparing the Land

Imagine you are on a huge rocky island with no grass, trees, animals, or other human beings. The only sounds you hear are those of the wind whistling and the waves breaking on the jagged shoreline. This lonely place was Vermont millions of years ago.

Lots of changes have taken place since those lonely days. Nature has worked for hundreds of millions of years to carve out the land of rounded mountains and gentle valleys that is now known as Vermont. Gradually the resources of our land were blended into beautiful and useful rocks, and the landscape was carpeted with green forests. How did these amazing changes take place? Go back in your mind for a moment to the barren land that existed millions of years ago. The wind and the waves breaking on the jagged shoreline gradually splintered the rocks into smaller sediments. This action is called erosion. As the sediments began to build up, they formed into layers and later hardened into rocks. Rocks formed in this manner are called sedimentary rocks. One sedimentary rock found in Vermont is slate, which comes in various colors, including green, red, chocolate, and gray. Today most of Vermont's slate is located in the Taconic region (see map on page 4).

As the land went through many more changes, Vermont's famous granite was pushed to the surface by underground pressure. Granite is an igneous rock (rock that is melted by great heat within the earth and later cooled and hardened). Millions of years after it was formed, humans found this rock in many places on the eastern side of our state. Today we call these regions the Eastern Foothills and the Northeastern Highlands.

During this rock-building time, another beautiful rock called marble was formed. Marble is a metamorphic rock (formed by great heat and pressure). The great heat of volcanic activity and the pressure of the moving land pressed and heated the limestone into multicolored marble. It is found mostly to the west of the Green Mountains in the Valley of Vermont and the Champlain Lowlands.

Gradually the Green Mountains were pushed up like a backbone running north and south through the center of the region. The Taconic Mountains were formed in the southwestern section. Both these mountain ranges were tall and rocky like the Alps and may have been as high as fifteen thousand feet!

Note

Scientists refer to early Lake Champlain as the Champlain Sea because it was an arm of the Atlantic Ocean and composed of salt water.

Animals began to inhabit the land and waters of the region. Reptiles known as plesiosaurs (plē'·zē·ō·sors), believed by some to be ancestors of Champ, the Champlain monster, swam in the Champlain Sea. They had a small head, long neck, and wide body with four flipperlike limbs and a long tail. Plants also began to grow on the land.

After millions of years, the earth entered an Ice Age. It became so cold that winter snows never melted and a layer of ice and snow, up to twenty thousand feet thick, covered the land that would become Vermont. This ice wall is known as a glacier. Its great weight

Physiographic Regions of Vermont

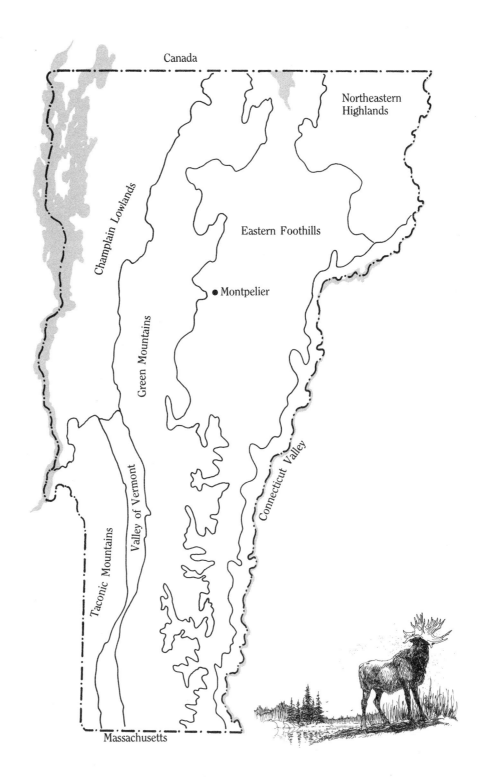

Inset

Cervalces: extinct moose-elk

(Courtesy Grace Brigham)

From Walter G. Ellison, A Guide to Birdfinding in Vermont *(Woodstock, Vermont: Vermont Institute of Natural Sciences, 1981.) Reprinted by permission of the Vermont Institute of Natural Sciences.*

moved over the rocky mountains at a snail's pace, grinding the jagged peaks into rounded tops and crushing all plants and trees in its path.

After thousands of years, the climate began to warm up again, and the glacier started to melt. In the many depressions formed by the weight of the glacier, melting ice created cold, clear lakes. The melting glacier also revealed that great valleys had been carved on both sides of the state. What would become the Connecticut River Valley originally was a series of glacial lakes. As the barriers between the lakes eroded, the 407-mile river was formed.

Vermont's western body of water, known as the Champlain Sea, grew enormously in the Champlain Lowlands. Twelve thousand years ago, the sea was salty and covered 20,500 square miles. As the land rose up after the glacier left, the lake slowly shrank to what it is today, about 490 square miles of water.

The rotting plants and trees mixed with the existing sediments to form fertile soil called humus. As the warming trend advanced over the state, spruce and fir trees began to grow in this fertile soil. Large mammals such as elk, musk ox, mastodons, and caribou began to browse in the sparse forests for food. In this environment, new beings came to live and hunt: humans. Their artifacts have been found scattered throughout the state, mostly in the Champlain Valley and the river valleys.

Paleoindians

The ancient people who first came to live and hunt in our valleys are called Paleo-indians. *Palaios* is the Greek word for "ancient." They are the ancestors of the present-day Native Americans.

Note

Archaeologists are scientists who study the lives and cultures of ancient people by examining their material remains.

Many archaeologists believe that these first people came to this continent over a land bridge from Asia, following a path that cut through two ice masses formed during the Ice Age. They call this path the MacKenzie Corridor and believe that people gradually migrated through this corridor following animals that were searching for food.

Many Native Americans, however, believe that their ancient ancestors originated on this continent. Most scientists agree that millions of years ago, all the continents started out as one huge continent called Pangaea, or "all earth." Native American tradition holds that their ancestors began life on that section of Pangaea that would later become North America.

Note

"To migrate" means to move from one place to another to live.

The Paleoindians made their way to Vermont about eleven thousand years ago. Small groups of families lived together in caves or shelters made out of skins and saplings. They hunted big game such as elk, caribou, and perhaps mastodons. Archaeologists have just recently begun to piece together the story of these prehistoric hunters in Vermont, and it is still sketchy. Much more is known about their descendants, who have come to be known as the Abenaki.

The Abenaki

Sometime in our shadowy past, the giant mammals that once roamed our state disappeared. They either became extinct or migrated north into Canada as the forests began to thicken. Towering pines grew to six feet around and two hundred feet high and became the habitat for smaller mammals, such as deer, rabbits, and squirrels.

In such surroundings, a new culture developed. The people discovered different ways to use the woodlands for their survival. Gradually they developed new weapons to hunt the smaller animals and new tools with which to farm. Housing and clothing styles changed through the years, much as our styles continue to change today.

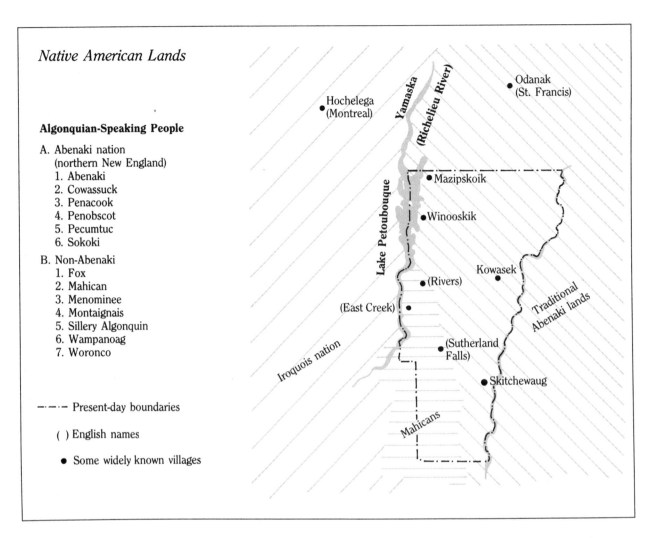

Native American Lands

Algonquian-Speaking People

A. Abenaki nation
   (northern New England)
   1. Abenaki
   2. Cowassuck
   3. Penacook
   4. Penobscot
   5. Pecumtuc
   6. Sokoki

B. Non-Abenaki
   1. Fox
   2. Mahican
   3. Menominee
   4. Montaignais
   5. Sillery Algonquin
   6. Wampanoag
   7. Woronco

–·–·– Present-day boundaries

( ) English names

● Some widely known villages

By about four thousand years ago, the people of what is today northern New England and lower Canada had joined together to form a great nation called the Alnôbak nation. Today they are called Abenaki—the people.

This nation was composed of many tribes. The people who lived in what is now Vermont were the western Abenaki, except for the Mahicans, who lived in the southwestern part of the region. The tribes of the nation had different languages and customs but also many things in common. In the rest of this unit, we will explore some of the customs common among the people of the Abenaki nation. We also will watch the coming of the white people through their eyes and try to imagine what it was like to be an Abenaki when whites first appeared in the forests.

Abenaki Village Life

Permanent villages dotted the land on high bluffs near rivers and lakes. Many families (a tribe) lived together in each village in bark-covered houses. They built their homes by tying large slabs of bark together and covering a sapling frame. They covered the inside walls with another layer of bark. Up to four families shared a house. Each family had its own compartment with a smoke hole, a hearth, and a storage pit. The families in one house were all related to each other.

The life of the Abenaki was centered on the changing seasons. Summer, fall, winter, and spring were the occasions for different hunting, fishing, gathering, and recreational

A family sugaring scene among the Abenaki (Courtesy Grace Brigham)

activities. Vermonters of today still have seasonal activities. See whether you can find any similarities as we follow the Abenaki through a typical year in their lives.

During the coldest part of the winter, the tribe stayed in the village. The women made new clothes, sewed moccasins, and decorated them with porcupine quills. The men repaired or made new tools and weapons. When the snow was deep, the people moved about on snowshoes. The winter was a relaxing time when relatives visited each other and much socializing and storytelling went on around the campfire.

Sometime in February, when the coldest part of the winter was over, the people celebrated with a midwinter feast. Everyone danced and played games. The amount of food eaten depended on how much was left in storage from the fall.

After the feast, the main hunting season began. Families separated from the tribe and traveled to their upland hunting territory, somewhere within the traditional tribal lands. The Abenaki called their territory *ndakinna*, "our land," and felt very close to it. Ndakinna had been in their families for generations and was essential to their way of life. It was so important that buying and selling of ndakinna was unheard of.

Ndakinna provided the people with just about everything they needed. During the main hunting season, the men hunted the many animals that shared the forests with the Abenaki. By this time, they had invented the bow and arrow and used it skillfully during the hunt. Fresh venison stew tasted delicious after a winter of eating dried meat. The women prepared the animal skins for blankets and clothing. They saved the bones for decorations, jewelry, and tools. Threads and ropes came from the tendons.

When spring arrived, the families returned to their village for fishing, fowling, and plant gathering. The men fished for salmon and shad, which were abundant at this time of year as they migrated upstream to spawn. Many birds, such as geese, ducks, gulls, and the now-extinct passenger pigeons, also were on the move.

During this time, the women prepared for maple sugaring by putting diagonal cuts in the trees and placing chips at the ends to direct the flow into birch-bark pails. Everyone pitched in to help collect the sap in large troughs. Later they filled green birch-bark kettles or pottery containers and boiled the sap over hot embers. Soon the sweet smell of boiling maple sugar filled the spring air. The first spring taste of sugar was as enjoyable then as it is today. Later in the spring, the women gathered young ferns and other plants while singing personal gathering songs.

When it was warm enough, in April or May, the planting season began. The Abenaki planted maize (corn), beans, squash, and tobacco. Farming was not as important as hunting and gathering, but the vegetables added variety to their meals. The people carried on their hunting, fishing, and gathering activities throughout the summer. They gathered blackberries, raspberries, elderberries, butternuts, black walnuts, and hickory nuts. Along with other plants, these provided food and medicine for the people of the tribe.

Summer also was a good time for making pottery. Many hours were spent digging and cleaning the clay, which came from the earth. They removed rocks and pebbles and added water to make the clay workable. When they were happy with the shape of a pot, they added decorations. The last step was firing (heating) the pottery until it hardened. Archaeologists have found a few pots and many beautiful pottery shards made by the Abenaki long ago.

The crops were harvested in late summer and put away for the winter months, along with the dried meat and fish, berries, and nuts. At the end of the harvest, everyone celebrated at the harvest ceremonies.

In the fall, the families returned to their upland hunting territory to get a fresh supply of meat for the winter. They hunted rabbits, bobcat, squirrels, porcupines, deer, and other mammals. The moose hunt probably was the most exciting. The men were experts at mimicking the mating call of a moose through a rolled cone of birch bark. When a bull moose came crashing through the bushes, the hunter had to be alert and kill the huge animal quickly. If he was too slow, the hunter could be severely injured by an angry moose that could not find the female he thought had been calling him.

By the time the winter snows blanketed the ground, the people were back at their village. Food for the cold months was stored in the bark-lined pits of the family home, and everyone settled in for the long Vermont winter.

It is apparent from these Abenaki customs that family life was very important. They did, however, have contact with neighboring tribes and nations. Relations usually were friendly, with the exception of those with their long-time enemies, the Iroquois. The Abenaki called the Iroquois people "man-eaters," since they occasionally practiced cannibalism on their enemies. There was no love lost between the two nations, and they raided each other often across Lake Petoubouque (Champlain).

Before the Abenaki declared war on an enemy, they held a council meeting. Men, women, and children were allowed to speak on the matter, and everyone voted. In this way, the warriors knew that the whole tribe was behind them when they went into battle.

Trading was carried on among the friendly tribes during the summer months. It was an exciting time for the families traveling along the ancient forest paths to meet with other tribes. It was a time to get reacquainted with old friends and exchange new ideas and goods. Sometimes the goods came from as far away as the Great Lakes. Over the years, an extensive trading network developed.

White People Appear

The Abenaki continued to hunt, farm, and trade on their lands for centuries. Then something happened that would change their lives more rapidly than anything else in their memories. Imagine that one summer a group of Abenaki leaves its village to travel north to trade. On this particular trip, their trading partners introduce them to materials they have never seen before, including brass, iron, and wool. These new items generate much interest, just as new items in our stores cause us to be interested and curious.

The Abenaki do just as their ancestors had done for centuries: They accept the foreign materials and adapt them to their lives. What follows these items, however, will change the Abenaki culture as nothing had before. These objects come from white people, who will not be content to trade along the ancient paths but will follow their goods, looking for a place to settle. They will come with families and axes to cut down the majestic trees, and muskets and diseases that eventually will destroy many of the people whose ancestors had inhabited the forests for thousands of years.

These events did not happen all at once, however. The Abenaki continued to trade for the new goods, especially tools, woolen blankets, and cloth. Soon the whites themselves came far enough inland to trade in person. Imagine how the Abenaki felt when they first set eyes on these foreigners. (The first were Frenchmen.) Never before had they seen people with such light skin or dressed in such strange clothes. The foreigners' language sounded strange to the Abenaki's ears, and their customs were unfamiliar. It must have taken some time for the Abenaki to get used to these strangers in their land.

Unknown to anyone at first, the whites brought more than their goods to ndakinna. They also brought their diseases: plague, chicken pox, cholera, smallpox, measles, typhoid fever, and many others. The whites had been exposed to these diseases and had built up immunities; the Abenaki had not. Sickness raged through the villages, causing pain, fear, and death.

Note

An immunity is an internal protection against a disease.

Traditional medicines were tried on the diseases, but the *medalwinno*, or drum sound person, who had considerable power in dealing with familiar diseases, did not have as much luck with the new European ones. It takes much time to discover new cures, and these diseases moved through the villages very rapidly. Within one hundred years, as many as ninety percent of the people died. Great sorrow visited every family of ndakinna.

At the same time, the Abenaki noticed that the French people were not becoming sick and dying in the great numbers that the Abenaki were. The Abenaki were a very spiritual people and believed in the power of the Great Spirit. Many people believed that it was the white people's religion that saved them from this terrible nightmare. Partly for this reason, the Abenaki began to turn to Catholicism for their spiritual needs.

Through the years, the Abenaki built up good relations with their French neighbors. The French learned the Abenaki language and did not interfere with their basic way of life. They helped them militarily and even traded their muskets to the Abenaki, a very friendly sign.

But stories of another tribe of white people from the south soon reached the land of the Abenaki. This tribe was called the British. Native Americans from the south brought gruesome news of British massacres of entire tribes. Even women and children were killed while the warriors were away, terror tactics unheard of among the Abenaki. In time, they adopted this new tactic and used it against the British.

Note

A refugee is a person fleeing from his or her home to seek protection from danger.

As the British pushed their way onto the Abenaki lands, many refugees from the south left their traditional homes to live farther north. One of these refugees was a man named Grey Lock from the Woronoco tribe. He came to live in the Abenaki village

These are Indians of lower Canada, probably Abenaki. By 1662, the Abenaki from all over Vermont were traveling as far as Montreal for Catholic church services. (Lithograph by Cornelius Krieghoff, Courtesy C–56 Public Archives of Canada)

on the Missisquoi around 1712. He and others brought tales of terror about the British to the people of ndakinna.

Grey Lock became a great war chief, leading raids against the British into what is now Massachusetts. For years, he and his warriors raided the British settlements that had grown up on their traditional lands. They raided during the spring, summer, and fall and returned to Missisquoi for the winter. British scouts and cavalry pursued Grey Lock, sometimes for months, but he never was caught. Once he even trailed a British scouting party while they were looking for him!

Finally, in March 1726, the warring tribes signed a treaty with the British. Grey Lock did not trust the British and refused to sign it. Poised to begin another season of raiding in the Otter Valley of Massachusetts, he nevertheless returned peacefully to Missisquoi. That village became his home until he died sometime in the 1740s.

Meanwhile, the Abenaki gave the French permission to build small settlements on ndakinna. In 1754, a great war was declared between the French and British tribes. Naturally, the Abenaki helped their friends the French. Together, they raided the British forts and settlements to the south.

In 1759, the British sent Major Robert Rogers on a journey from Crown Point up Lake Petoubouque to search for and destroy Abenaki villages. (See the map on page 6.) This raid usually is reported in history books as an outstanding victory for Rogers and his Rangers in which two hundred to three hundred Abenaki were killed. That is because the British believed Rogers's report upon his return. French records and Abenaki oral traditions, however, tell a very different story.

The people of Mazipskoik had moved away from their village to another site deep within their territory. They frequently did this during times of war to avoid enemy attacks. On October 4, some Abenaki, who had stayed to watch the village, discovered Rogers and his Rangers canoeing up the lake. They watched the British from the trees. When Rogers found no one at Mazipskoik, the Rangers moved inland toward the village at Odanak. The watching Abenaki destroyed the Rangers' canoes after they had gone.

As Rogers moved north, one of his Mahican scouts secretly ran ahead and warned the people of Odanak of the advancing British. Many Odanak warriors were hunting at the time. The older men and women tried to gather the children and hide outside the village before Rogers arrived. Many—but not all—escaped. Rogers and his Rangers attacked the village, killing thirty people, mostly women and children. The Rangers burned the village, destroying everything, including seventy-year-old church records. When the Abenaki warriors returned to their burned-out homes and dead wives and children, they had no time to mourn. Immediately, they pursued the British across ndakinna, killing many of the Rangers. Other Rangers died of starvation, as they were forced to walk back to Crown Point and had no provisions to feed themselves.

After the destruction of their village, the people of Odanak were scattered for many years. Eight years later, they rebuilt their village, and Odanak became a refuge for people driven from their land by the British. Even many years later, as Americans pushed west, members of western tribes came to Missisquoi and Odanak for refuge.

The people of Missisquoi returned to their village after the war between the French and the British. The French had lost, and the British began moving into ndakinna in greater numbers. A few French and Dutch settlers respected the Abenaki rights to the land and rented pieces of it. The British, however, believed that the land belonged to them because they had won the war. The British king gave the Abenaki land to British governors, who gradually sold it to others. Two men named Ira and Levi Allen bought the land now called Swanton and told the Abenaki they had no right to live there anymore.

The Abenaki appealed to the British authorities but were told they had no right to the land because they were "wanderers." The British obviously did not understand the traditional Abenaki way of life. The people who had lived on ndakinna for thousands of years knew they could no longer fight the white tribe—there were too many and they were too powerful. Some moved to Odanak, which was already very crowded. Most, however, refused to leave and simply disappeared into the forest, as they had during the war.

As more and more white settlers came and their towns grew, the Abenaki adopted many of the European ways. They spoke English, dressed like Europeans, and lived in European type houses. But inside they remained Abenaki. They adapted to their new world but carried on many of their traditional customs.

In the twentieth century, the descendants of these Abenaki who "disappeared" from Vermont have reasserted their rights. They believe that they have traditional rights to the land and the game that are different from those of European descent. They are finding their own way to live without conforming to every aspect of the white ways. We shall explore what native Vermonters are doing to assert their rights in Section III.

Activity

A Pottery-Making Activity (18)

Using Vermont clay to make pots was a traditional Abenaki craft. Try your hand at making your own pottery in the traditional way. The most common method was the coil method described here.

1. After cleansing the clay, the Abenaki added "temper" to prevent it from shrinking or cracking during firing. Many things were used for temper, including crushed quartz, bone, limestone, and fine river-washed gravel. Three parts clay to one part temper was a common mixture.

2. Next, a round, flat disc was made and the edges bent up to form a shallow cone or bowl shape. This was the base of the pot. Long coils were made and spiraled around the base to form the sides. The top of the pot was made straight or curved inward or outward. Lips were flattened or left rounded. Sometimes the lips were scalloped or castellated (built with turrets, like a castle).

3. Then the coils were smoothed together with a flat river stone and a paddle made from a piece of wood or a cord-wrapped stick. Once the coils were fused together and the desired surface finish achieved, decorations were applied. Carved wood and stone pieces, pointed sticks, shells, fabric, netting, and cord-wrapped sticks were pressed into the clay, creating many different designs. Sometimes decorated collars were applied around the rim of a pot. The lip and interior of the rim also were decorated by some Abenaki.

4. The pottery was then ready for firing. A hot fire was built and left to burn until a bed of ashes and coals remained. The pots were placed in the fire, with ashes and coals heaped around and over them. After many hours, the fire was left to burn out, and the pots cooled. Some of the pots turned gray or black; others turned tan or orange, depending on the type of clay used and the conditions of firing. After firing, the pots became strong and hard.

Using native clay or modeling clay, follow the above steps in making your own pot. You may want to use a modern oven to fire your pot. Here are some ideas for decorations that the Abenaki used:

= Rocker Stamp

= Shell Impressed

= Reed Punctate (use reeds or drinking straws)

= Check Stamp

= Incised Line

= Fabric Impressed

= Cord-Wrapped Stick (use rope or yarn)

= Iroquois Castellations (Archaeologists have attributed these to the Iroquois, but the Abenaki made this type of design, too.)*

*From *Vermont's Original Inhabitants* by Pam Currance. Reprinted by permission of Vermont Historical Society.

Recipe

Pemmican
(traditional Native American food)

your favorite meat (wild or store bought)
½ pint vinegar
2 cups salt
2 tablespoons pepper
your favorite berries (cranberries taste great)
A-1 sauce (optional)

1. Cut the meat into strips (across the grain) about ¼ inch thick.
2. Boil the meat in two quarts of water, the vinegar, and the salt and pepper for about 5 minutes.
3. Remove meat from liquid and roll flat with a rolling pin. If the juices are red, it needs more boiling. The meat should be gray-brown and somewhat rubbery.
4. Put the strips on an oven rack, allowing space in between them. Set the oven at 200°F and cook for about 1½ hours. Keep the oven door open a crack to allow moisture to escape. Remove the meat when it is almost dry.
5. (Optional) To add a little extra flavor, "paint" the strips with A-1 sauce.
6. Crush the meat and add an equal amount of berries. Grind everything together. Keep some in a deerskin pouch (or plastic bag). This food can be chewed for an hour and is very tasty and nutritious.*

Recipe

Toasted Pumpkin or Squash Seeds

1. Spread seeds on a baking sheet.
2. Sprinkle with oil, salt, or herbs.
3. Roast in the oven at 325°F or cook over an open fire.
4. After about 20 minutes, remove from heat, cool, and store in airtight containers.

Game

Iroquois Dart Game
(played by the neighboring nation to our west)

Two even teams—played out of doors

Each player has a wooden spear or dart, about 4 feet long. An umpire rolls a hoop made out of reeds (or a Hula-Hoop) in front of a team. The first player tries to throw the spear through the hoop as it is moving. If (s)he succeeds, the next player tries. If (s)he fails, the other team tries until someone fails. The first team with everyone getting the spears through wins.

*Adapted from activities by Norman Weis and Jim Howard, Regional Center for Educational Training, Hanover, N.H.

Story

Mazipskoik: Abenaki village at the mouth of the Missisquoi River

The first ray of sunlight filtered through the smoke hole of the bark-covered lodge. Kisosis (Little Sunshine) was already awake. She was excited about gathering berries with her mother today. For the first time, she would carry her own basket. She crept out of bed and looked down the earthen hall to see if anyone was getting up. Gray spirals of smoke floated upward as the women began building cooking fires. Children began scampering in and out of the lodge.

Soon Kisosis was helping her mother boil water. Sôpi (Sophie), her sister of three summers, ran by and upset the soapstone pot filled with water. The fire hissed, but no one uttered a sound. Children were not scolded because it might crush their spirit. If parents had a very unruly child, they would isolate him or her from the family. The child's face would be blackened, and he or she would be put outside alone. But this treatment was rarely needed.

Kisosis picked up the clay water pot and walked to the great river. She looked at the still, dark forest that lay beyond the village and could hardly wait to begin the berrying trip. She filled the pot and quickly returned to her lodge with the water.

Her brother, Tmakwasis (Little Beaver), was playing with his bow and arrow. "Nitsemiz (my little brother) handles the bow well," Kisosis said to her mother.

"You're right," answered Pagôn (Butternut). "Soon he'll be practicing on the moving target."

When the meal was ready, the family sat down to eat ground nut cakes, berries, and black drink. Afterward, her father, Soaring Hawk, joined the men and older boys to make new tools. New spear points and scrapers were needed for the moose-hunting trip they soon would be taking.

Kisosis's grandmother sat with the older women sewing new moccasins out of the last of the moosehide. She would line them with soft rabbit fur and decorate them with porcupine quills. The younger children played nearby.

Finally, the other women and girls picked up their baskets made from corn shucks and entered the woods. Kisosis breathed in the freshness of the forest as her moccasins stepped noiselessly along the pine-covered ground. Her heart beat quickly against her chest. She wanted so much to make her first gathering a success. She moved into a thicket to her right. Her steps quickened as she saw large blackberries hanging from the bushes.

Suddenly she stopped. In the thicket with her were two small bear cubs eating the berries. She felt the blood drain from her head. Their mother must be nearby, she thought. Kisosis felt as if she had grown roots and become one of the pine trees in the forest. She could not move.

Then she heard grunting and branches breaking up ahead. Still she could not move. She prayed to the Great Bear Spirit to forgive her for coming to this spot. Her legs were weakening with fear: She could not protect herself from a bear. Then, slowly, the cubs ambled away from her to join their mother. Kisosis stayed motionless for what seemed like a long time, till she was sure the bears were gone. Then she very carefully and quietly backed out of the thicket. When her legs felt strong enough, she ran through the trees to join the others.

They had not even noticed that she was not with them. After she told them what had happened, everyone murmured in wonder. "Your prayers were very powerful!" Clay Basket said.

"Awahsos (the bear) has honored you by giving you his protection," her mother said. During the rest of the morning, Kisosis was careful not to leave the group. They found many berries, and everyone filled her own basket. But such success could not make Kisosis forget how helpless she had felt in the face of the bears. She promised herself it would not happen again. When she returned to the village, she would begin learning how to use a bow and arrow. It would have to be in secret, though, because women were not supposed to use hunting tools. When she was good enough, she would show her secret. They would *have* to allow her to carry the weapons during gathering trips once they saw how good she was.

When the gathering was finished and they were on their way back to the village, her mother spoke to her. "You have done well. There will be feasting when we return."

Kisosis knew that she must not eat any of her berries. After the first successful gathering, one must offer everything to her family and friends. The same would be true for Tmakwasis on his first successful hunt.

When they returned to the lodge, some silver-skinned skohtam (trout) were hanging from the rafters waiting to be cleaned by the women. Kisosis could imagine her father standing motionless on the mossy, overhanging bank with his spear poised over the pool in the river. At the flash of a trout, he would thrust his spear into the water and pull it out with a fish on the end.

That evening, everyone feasted on fish, pond lily roots, and berries. Kisosis was praised for her bravery with the bears and her success in gathering so many juicy berries. At the end of the meal, Pagôn had an announcement. "Now I must give you a new name, one more fitting for you after this day. From now on you will be called Malian (Marion). We can't call you 'little' anymore."

Her heart filled with pride: She loved her new name! Now she would not have a baby name anymore. She smiled widely at everyone.

After dinner, the girls played double ball. They used a curved stick to try and toss the ball into a net. The boys played a hoop game in which someone rolls a hoop, while the rest try to throw a pole through it.

When the sun cast its last rays over the mountains across the great water, Petoubouque, the children entered the lodge and went to bed. Malian wanted to stay up, but she was very tired after her exciting day. She fell asleep wondering what new name she would get when she learned how to use the bow and arrow. Her dreams were filled with the wonderful adventures she would have with her new skills.

UNIT 2

The First Europeans: French and Dutch

Let's go back in time in our minds and try to imagine our state in the early 1600s. The forests that grew after the melting of the glacier still shelter the land. Pine trees are six feet around and two hundred feet tall, growing in such abundance that sunlight cannot reach the soil. The trails of the Abenaki cut through the forests, across old decaying trees and past lavish mushrooms scattered on the forest floor. Patches of sunlight warm the ground where villages have been built and garden plots cultivated by the people who have lived and prospered here for ten thousand years.

One day new faces appear in the forests. They are the faces of white people who have come to explore the land and gain riches from selling the skins of the forest animals to others of their kind. We have already seen the arrival of these new people through the eyes of the Abenaki. In this unit, we will follow these first Europeans who came to live and trap in the forests and experience their arrival from their point of view.

The French arrived in North America in the 1500s, spreading south along the St. Lawrence and Richelieu rivers. The first Dutch explorers arrived in the early 1600s and spread north along the Hudson River. Both countries claimed what is now Vermont.

The experiences of these French and Dutch explorers and immigrants were quite similar. Their main reasons for coming to this continent were to trap and trade in order to increase their economic power among the other European countries. They both realized they needed the help of the native people, so they kept settlements small to avoid antagonizing them.

Since they both arrived in North America at about the same time, you would think that the Dutch and the French would clash someday, but instead they were both defeated by the English.

The French

The French called their new trading and trapping territory New France. They developed successful trading networks with the Abenaki and gradually built forts along the water-ways to protect their trading posts.

In 1609, Samuel de Champlain and two other Frenchmen canoed onto Lake Petoubouque (renamed Champlain) guided by members of the Abenaki nation. This ordinary canoe trip had far-reaching effects on the history of our state because of a skirmish with a group of Iroquois. The Iroquois and Abenaki nations were bitter enemies. During the canoe trip, Champlain and his companions came upon a group of Iroquois. A battle broke out during which the French used their muskets to help their friends the Abenaki defeat their enemy. From that time on, the Iroquois vowed to fight the French and sided with the English in future battles. Thankful for the victory, the Abenaki vowed to help the French. The battle lines had been drawn!

Samuel de Champlain and fellow explorers arriving in North America to begin trading with the Abenaki (Painting by Charles W. Jeffery, Courtesy C-103059 Public Archives of Canada)

Gradually, the French began to inch their way into Vermont. By the 1640s, they had cleared enough of the forests to establish trading sites near the mouths of the Winooski River and La Rivière aux Loutres (River of the Otters). Besides trading, the French were deeply interested in converting the Indians to Catholicism. They brought priests with them wherever they went. The traders also relished the fact that the priests told the Abenaki it was a sin to trade with the Protestant English.

In 1665, Sieur (Captain) La Motte was sent to an island in northern Lake Champlain to build a new fort in an attempt to subdue the Iroquois. (This island later became known as Isle LaMotte.) Completed in 1666, Fort Ste. Anne was the first fort in Vermont. The chapel built for the men was dedicated to Saint Anne and was the first church in the state.

Note

Ste. is the French abbreviation for Sainte, denoting a female saint.

Six hundred soldiers trekked through the forests and traveled the waterways to man the fort. By that first winter, the Iroquois appeared to be at peace, and most of the soldiers were withdrawn to Montreal. Only sixty men were left to spend the winter on the frigid island. Unfortunately, provisions ran short long before the spring reinforcements arrived. Vinegar meant to supply vitamins had leaked from the casks. Kegs of brandy sent from France to warm the men on freezing winter nights had been drunk by the sailors during the voyage and replaced with sea water. The soldiers at Fort Ste. Anne were reduced to eating only bread and bacon.

Before long, forty of the men fell sick with scurvy and many eventually died. The remaining soldiers lit fires in all the huts to make it appear as if many soldiers were there. The Iroquois did not attack. Perhaps they had been tricked, but more likely

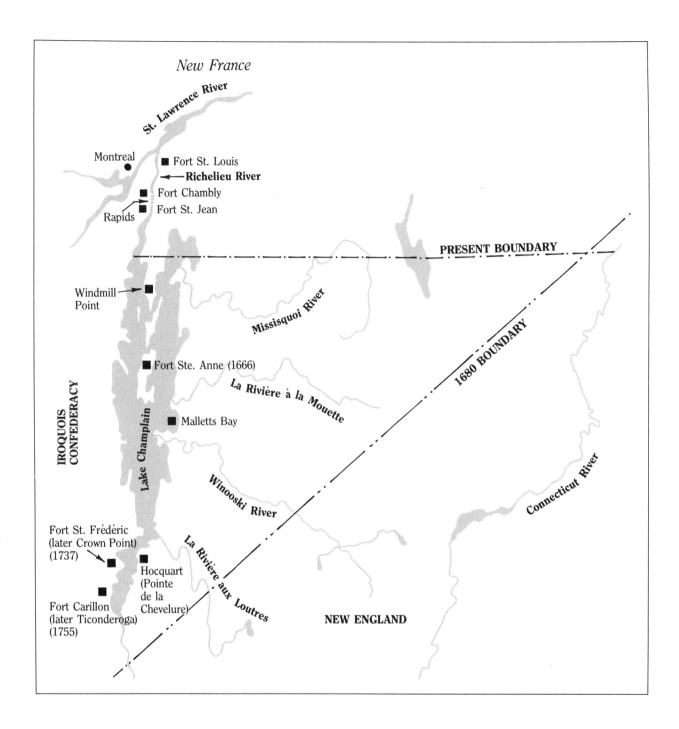

New France

St. Lawrence River

Montreal

■ Fort St. Louis

◄—**Richelieu River**

■ Fort Chambly

■ Fort St. Jean

Rapids

PRESENT BOUNDARY

Windmill → ■
Point

Missisquoi River

1680 BOUNDARY

■ Fort Ste. Anne (1666)

La Rivière à la Mouette

IROQUOIS CONFEDERACY

■ Malletts Bay

Lake Champlain

Winooski River

Connecticut River

Fort St. Frédéric
(later Crown Point)
(1737) → ■   ■

Hocquart
(Pointe
de la
Chevelure)

La Rivière aux Loutres

■

Fort Carillon
(later Ticonderoga)
(1755)

NEW ENGLAND

they were just not interested in waging war during the winter. Provisions finally arrived to save the remaining weak and tattered soldiers.

A short time after Fort Ste. Anne was built, it was abandoned and burned. Historians believe that other forts took over the job of Fort Ste. Anne, but no one knows for sure why it was burned.

The French continued to move into Vermont and built outposts for their trading ventures at Windmill Point (Alburg), Malletts Bay, and Hocquart (Chimney Point).

Settlement

Note

In a feudal system, a noble owned the land and rented it to serfs (peasants). The serfs supplied labor and grain. In return the noble protected them from enemies. The serfs could never hope to own the land.

Small settlements that resembled the European feudal system grew up around the out-posts. The king of France granted pieces of land to seigneurs (nobles), who owed allegiance to the king. The seigneurs were expected to attract settlers who would pay rent to the landowners. If their land remained unsettled, they had to give it back to the king. Because of this restriction, the seigneurs often offered tools, provisions, and even free rent to persuade people from France and New France to settle the land.

The first successful seigneur owned land at the southern end of Lake Champlain. He persuaded a group of farmers to start a settlement across from Fort St. Frédéric in the 1730s on the site of an old Dutch trading post. It was named Hocquart and was the first white settlement in Vermont. A Swedish naturalist exploring the area many years later found apples, plums, and currants planted there by the settlers. In the DAR (Daughters of the American Revolution) Park in Addison, a stone marker stands on the former location of one of Hocquart's cabins. Very little evidence remains to indicate the size of this settlement.

This and other small settlements in Vermont thrived until 1755. At that time, the French and the English, who had been fighting off and on for years, began the French and Indian War, which would leave New France in the hands of the English. At that time, the wives and children of many of the Frenchmen who fought in the war moved back to Canada to avoid attacks by the English or their Iroquois allies.

After years of fighting, the final defeat of the French in North America took place in a bloody battle on the Plains of Abraham near Quebec City in 1759. After the English victory, the French reluctantly gave up Canada and all their lands east of the Mississippi River.

Although the French government was ousted, some French settlers stayed in Vermont. One of the better known was Captain Mallette, who lived for many years on the bay later named for him. Scholars have suggested that some French families might have lived in remote hill sections and were not noticed by the English. Their descendants may be sitting next to you in your classroom today.

Building the State

Each ethnic group that lived in Vermont helped to build our state into what it is today. It is sometimes difficult to pinpoint exactly what each group contributed, but there are some clues. Names are obvious ones. Many of the place names in Vermont remain as a reminder of our French heritage.

Long-lasting ties with France and Canada are other clues. Because of continuing hostility toward the English, Frenchmen from France and Canada fought with the Americans during the American Revolution. Much of our French heritage is linked to the descendants of the original French settlers who flowed to Vermont from Canada in the next century. In Section II, you will read about the thousands of French Canadians who immigrated to Vermont during the nineteenth century to farm and work in our industries. Because our country welcomed so many immigrants, France presented the United States with the Statue of Liberty in 1884.

Activity

Model of Fort Ste. Anne (18,20)

Excavations have been done at the fort since the Catholic Church bought the site in the 1870s. The original fort was 96 feet by 144 feet and was surrounded by a double palisade 15 feet tall. Many dirt mounds covered remnants of walls, fireplaces, a brick oven, and French and Indian artifacts. Use these directions to construct a model of the first fort in Vermont.

You will need:

empty detergent or cereal boxes
old newspapers
brown modeling clay (brown paint is optional)
dishwashing liquid
3½-inch sticks gathered from the woods
corrugated paper or toothpicks
thick cardboard for the base

1. Lay the cereal boxes down to cover the base. Glue them to each other and to the base.
2. Soak several newspapers in water with a little dishwashing liquid for about 5 minutes. Squeeze the water out of the paper and lay it over the boxes to cover completely.
3. Soften some clay with water and spread it thinly over the wet paper. Make it bumpy to look like real ground. (Or you may paint the paper to look like ground.)
4. Make snakelike shapes out of clay and lay them on the ground in a 2- by 3-foot rectangle. Put the clay at the corners in the shape of bastions.

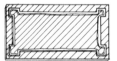

5. Place a double palisade of sticks into the clay border to form the walls of the fort.
6. Build a small barracks, a chapel, and a cooking house out of sticks, corrugated paper, or toothpicks. Place them inside the fort.
7. Finish with dirt, moss, and other materials to simulate bushes, trees, and other aspects of the natural environment.

The Dutch

During the early 1600s, when the French were busy exploring and settling the north, the Dutch began explorations farther to the south. The Dutch West India Company was looking for a good place to set up a trading post. In 1624, they bought Manhattan Island from the Indians and began the settlement of New Amsterdam (later renamed New York). They claimed all of the East Coast north of them, including Vermont, and

Note

"Inquisition" comes from the word "inquiry." Leaders of the Catholic Church in Spain and Portugal, who were very powerful in the government, questioned under torture non-Catholics. Many people were killed for their religion because they were seen as a threat to the Church's power.

called it New Netherlands. The Dutch West India Company encouraged small settlements to strengthen their hold on the land.

While most of the settlers were Protestant, some of the earliest ones were Jewish. They had lived under Dutch rule in Brazil (South America). When the Portuguese conquered Brazil in 1654, however, they brought the Inquisition with them. The Jews were ordered to convert to Catholicism or leave the country. Most returned to Holland, where they enjoyed religious freedom, but a small group migrated to New Amsterdam. They probably were the first Jewish people to settle in North America.

While New Amsterdam was a successful settlement, many others were not. By 1664, the English settlements were much more numerous. They easily defeated the Dutch and assumed control over much of New Netherlands, renaming it New England. Although the government became English, the Dutch people stayed and gradually made their way to Vermont.

Settlement

The small Dutch settlements resembled the European feudal system, just as the French settlements had. The Dutch West India Company offered large pieces of land to anyone who would finance fifty settlers. These financiers were called patroons. The settlers owed perpetual rent to the patroons and their descendants. When the English took over, the New York territory was settled in a similar manner: The settlers had to rent the land. (In Massachusetts and Connecticut, the settlers had the choice of owning or renting. See Unit 3 for problems arising out of these different ways of settling the land.)

In 1688, Governor Thomas Dongan of New York sold a piece of land for a town in the Pownal area. (The map on page 28 shows that much of Vermont was claimed by New York at that time.) By 1724, a Dutch settlement was thriving in Pownal. Dutch people already had settled around Emerald Lake, Highgate, and Swanton. In 1732, John Lydius, a Dutchman, obtained a deed to land bordered on the north by Otter Creek and covering large parts of Addison and Rutland counties. He seems to have been a shady character, and no one is sure how he obtained the deed from the Indians. Over the years, other Dutch families came to Vermont. In this century, the newest Dutch settlers have started farms in the Vergennes area.

Building the State

When the Dutch came to Vermont more than two hundred fifty years ago, they tended to build small farms near streams (unlike other settlers who avoided the streams and built in the hills). The reason for this is that there were many more beavers then than there are today. Their dams caused the flood plains to be much wetter and provided cleared meadows for farms. The Dutch were used to the wet land, since it was like the Netherlands from which they had emigrated. Their farms in the lowlands continue to be used today, while many of the hillside farms built by other ethnic groups have been abandoned.

Note

"To emigrate" means to leave your homeland and settle in another country.

A study of the architecture in Vermont also shows a Dutch legacy. If you look at buildings near you, you may find gambrel and bell-shaped roofs, dormers, and crow stepping. Long, squat barns also are reminiscent of the Dutch style. (See the activity on architecture on page 22.)

So far in this section, we have seen the land that will become Vermont change from a sparsely inhabited wilderness to the land of the Abenaki. After many centuries, the Abenaki met white people called the French and the Dutch, who called the land New France and New Netherlands. The next name change—to New England—has stayed to this day. In the next unit, we will meet the English settlers who flowed into Vermont following the defeat of the French and the Dutch.

Activity

Dutch Architecture   (1, 12)

Take a walk on the streets and roads near your school. Watch for buildings that look like these sketches. Keep track of how many of each type you see.

1. Gambrel roof with dormers

2. Bell-shaped roof

3. Dormers embellished with curves

4. Crow stepping on roof

5. Squat barn, the width, height, and length of which are almost equal

Back at school, make a graph showing the number of buildings you saw and the number of buildings with each of the above characteristics. Summarize the Dutch architectural influence in your area based on the graph.

Recipe

Croques Monsieur
(French)

You will need:

loaf of French bread
sliced ham
Swiss cheese
eggs, beaten
butter

1. Cut loaf lengthwise. Fill with ham and cheese.
2. Cut loaf into sandwich-size pieces. Dip into eggs.
3. Fry sandwiches in melted butter until golden and cheese has melted.

Recipe

Noodle-Apple Pudding
(Jewish tradition)*

You will need:

2 eggs
4 tablespoons sugar
¼ teaspoon salt
½ teaspoon cinnamon
1 cup grated apples
½ cup seedless raisins
4 cups cooked noodles
3 tablespoons melted butter

1. Beat the eggs and spices together.
2. Stir in fruit, noodles, and butter.
3. Put in greased baking dish. Bake at 400 °F for 40 minutes. Serves 8.

Game

My Great Aunt Lives in Tours
(Game From France)

Two or more players—indoors

Sit in a circle and repeat together:

    My great aunt lives in Tours,
    In a house with a cherry tree
    With a little mouse (squeak, squeak)
    . . .

Take turns adding other animals and other sounds until you cannot think of any more.
Repeat the whole jingle each time.
Samples:

    And a great big dog (bow wow)
    And a long fat snake (hiss, hiss)
    And a pink little pig (oink, oink)

You may want to learn animal names in French for the game.

*From Sally Innis Klitz, *The Jews* (Storrs, Conn.: The I.N. Thut World Education Center, 1980), p. 112. Reprinted by permission of the I.N. Thut World Education Center, The University of Connecticut, Storrs, Conn.

Game

Prooi (Captured)
(Game From the Netherlands)

For 8 or more players—indoors or out

The players pick pieces of paper out of a hat. On one piece is written "Prooi" (Prōoē). The lights are turned off, or everyone closes his or her eyes. The person who picked "Prooi" then hides. The players move around trying to find Prooi, keeping their eyes closed. When they touch one another, they say "Prooi?" The players who are *not* Prooi must answer, "Prooi?" The real Prooi gives no answer. He or she then takes the player who touched her or him by the hand, and they stand together silently. As other people find Prooi, they also join the group and do not answer when touched. Each child who finds the Prooi group must feel his or her way to the end of the line, not break into the middle. When no one is calling "Prooi?" the game is over. Everyone wins.

Story

Note
Mamam is the French Canadian word for mother. It is capitalized only at the beginning of a sentence.

Hocquart

Marcel was so excited he couldn't even talk. He sat in the middle of the dugout canoe that was gliding along Lake Champlain and stared at the thick forests on either side. His brother, Pierre, sat near him, while mamam and Papa paddled the canoe. After days of paddling down the Richelieu River and the lake and nights of camping in the woods and eating meals filled with wood ashes, they were finally near their new home.

Marcel's papa (Monsieur LaFleur) and some other men had come to this part of New France from Montreal a year ago to build their homes. They had picked a place near the stockade in case they needed help against the English or their Indian allies. The seigneur who owned the land had given them cornmeal and tools to help them get started. They built several cabins and a small church and called their settlement Hocquart.

"Are we almost there?" asked Marcel, pushing his light brown hair out of his eyes.

"Just a little way more," Papa replied. "Don't be so impatient."

"But I can't wait to see everything," Marcel said. He looked over the side into the deep blue water and sighed. *I guess I'll have to wait*, he thought impatiently. It was hard for him to contain his excitement after being forced to sit still for so long.

After what seemed like forever, the LaFleurs' canoe started angling toward the shore. "This must be it!" Pierre cried. The thrill in his voice matched Marcel's mood. As soon as the canoe beached on the crescent-shaped shore, he and Pierre ran up the steep bank. In a small clearing stood a log cabin. Behind the cabin was a forest of huge trees. It was so dark that Marcel could not see beyond the first few trees.

"Come and help unpack," mamam yelled up the bank.

As they walked up and down the bank unloading the canoe, Marcel wondered where the Indians lived. They had taught Papa how to grow beans, corn, and pumpkins. Papa had said that many Indians visited him during the winter he lived here alone. Papa said they were friendly and he enjoyed their company.

Finally, Marcel got a glimpse of the inside of the cabin. There was no door—just an old blanket covering the opening. Inside was one room with a loft up above. The big fireplace would easily keep the cabin warm in the winter. A large table stood in the middle of the room with wooden benches on both sides. A rope bed stood at the right. Underneath was a trundle bed, which would be pulled out at night for the boys.

Marcel started to unpack some things: horn cups, wooden plates, and blankets. They spent the rest of the day settling into their new cabin on the edge of the dark forest overlooking the lake. Once settled, they began planting crops, gathering berries and roots, and drying meat for winter.

One evening, Marcel and Pierre were carrying buckets of water to their pumpkin patch when they smelled a kettle of *samp* (porridge) cooking. Marcel was getting tired of samp and fish all the time. He longed for a cup of milk, but no farm animals could survive in the grassless forest. He hoped Papa would come back from hunting with a rabbit. Rabbit stew would be delicious. As they started back to the cabin, a new aroma wafted through the air. It was sweet.

"Smell that," Marcel said, inhaling.

"Mmmm, smells like maple sugar. Mamam must be sick of the plain old mush, too," Pierre answered.

They went inside and saw their mamam setting the boiling samp aside to cool. At that moment, they heard a strange noise outside. Everyone's ears perked up. Their senses had already become attuned to the everyday sounds and smells of the forest in which they lived. But this sound and smell were different from anything they had experienced. Their bodies automatically went on alert even before they knew in their minds what the danger was.

In the next instance, they knew. The blanket covering the doorway moved aside, and a bear stuck her head in. "Mon Dieu!" mamam cried. The boys opened their mouths in silent cries of alarm, not knowing what to do. "Quickly, up in the loft," said mamam, pushing the boys toward the ladder. All three scrambled up, and mamam pulled up the ladder after her.

From above, they watched the bear enter with two cubs and go straight for the samp. "She smelled the sugar, too," whispered Marcel. She picked up the kettle and drank some of the scalding samp. She immediately let out a roar and threw down the kettle. Her paws went into her mouth as if she was trying to get the samp out.

Pierre started laughing at the bear. When she heard him, she angrily tried to reach them in the loft. Pierre instantly quieted, and they all shrank back as far as they could. Marcel felt the blood drain from his head as he looked into the pained and angry eyes of the bear. He prayed to God to send the bear back into the forest.

After a few minutes of watching the bear flail at the loft and toss the table and benches around, Marcel's muscles were so tense they were almost paralyzed. Finally, the bear gave one last roar and left the cabin, her cubs trailing behind.

Silence filled the cabin. Marcel's muscles began to relax, and he became aware of his heart pumping furiously and blood surging to his head. Never had he been so scared. After a few minutes, they were all breathing easier, and mamam hugged the boys to her. "Thank God we're safe," she whispered.

"You're so dumb to laugh at the bear," Marcel said to Pierre when he found his voice again.

"How was I supposed to know the bear would get mad?" protested Pierre.

"This is no time to argue," said mamam, setting down the ladder. "We've got to clean this place up." They climbed down to start the chore, still shaky from the encounter. Marcel couldn't get the look in the bear's eyes out of his mind. He thought that animals must have the same feelings that people do.

He lifted a bench to put it back but found that it was broken. *The Indians are right about our being related to the animals,* he thought. *They get hurt and angry just like we do.*

Papa came home empty-handed from hunting, so the LaFleurs had very little to eat that night. Papa worked for hours making a sturdy slab door. He made wooden hinges to hang it on and would not go to bed until he was done.

When other settlers heard about the bears after Sunday Mass, some laughed; some called the bears vicious and stupid, but they all decided to add a wooden door to their cabins.

"We've got to do more than just build doors," Monsieur Mercier said.

"That's right," someone else yelled. "The whole community could be in danger." When they made plans to discuss the "savage beast," Marcel felt uneasy, but he wasn't sure why.

The LaFleur family started back through the forest toward their cabin. Marcel was awed, as always, by the huge trees, which wouldn't let the sun penetrate their denseness. As a result, the forest was dark and damp; mushrooms and moss grew everywhere, and rotting logs lay in all directions. It seemed like a magical, mysterious place to Marcel. A new thought suddenly occurred to him: *It's good that only a few Frenchmen have come to live in this place. Too many would disturb the peacefulness of the forest.* As he looked past the giant trees into the forest, he prayed it would always stay this way.*

*Sometime toward the end of the French and Indian War, Hocquart was abandoned and burned. The settlers returned to Canada. When the English arrived, they found only chimneys standing and named the place Chimney Point.

UNIT 3

From Grants to Republic to Statehood: British

The first British settlers to brave the unknown ocean and sail to New England came in 1620 on the Mayflower. Many more left Great Britain* in the years that followed, seeking freedom and land in North America. They had a difficult time surviving in our forests because they had little experience with the ways of the woods. In Britain, most forests had been chopped down long ago. Those that remained belonged to the king and nobles, and common people were not allowed to hunt in them.

Some Native Americans tried to help these strange white people survive in their new surroundings, but it took years for the Europeans to learn the ways of the forests. It took many more years for them to build familiar villages and towns in which they could feel safe and comfortable.

In the 1760s, something came over their descendants that would have amazed the original settlers. Young people who had grown up in the woods of Connecticut and Massachusetts and enjoyed the freedom of the forests began feeling hemmed in by the growing population. They began to look north to the still largely unsettled area between the Lake Champlain and Connecticut River valleys.

Unlike their ancestors, they were better at hunting and trapping and felt more at home in the woods. They yearned to escape the overcrowding of their towns. They looked to the north because the land was cheap and the trees were abundant for building homes. There were no taxes or other government or religious restrictions on their freedom. In this unit, we will explore with these young settlers as they forge a new state out of the northern wilderness.

Historical Background

Those first British settlers to move to the land now called Vermont in the 1760s bought their land from the governor of New Hampshire, Benning Wentworth. He sold his first grant of land in 1749 for the town of Bennington. No settlers arrived, however, until after the French and Indian War was over, as it would have been too dangerous to move there during the war.

This sale caused quite a stir in New York because the acting governor, Calderwalder Colden, believed that the land belonged to his colony. He knew that the original New York charter stated that the colony included the land west of Connecticut. At that time, that meant all the land west of the Connecticut River. So Colden wrote to the King of England complaining that Wentworth was selling his land.

*At that time, Great Britain was composed of England, Wales, Scotland, and Ireland. Today, England, Wales, Scotland, and Northern Ireland belong to Great Britain.

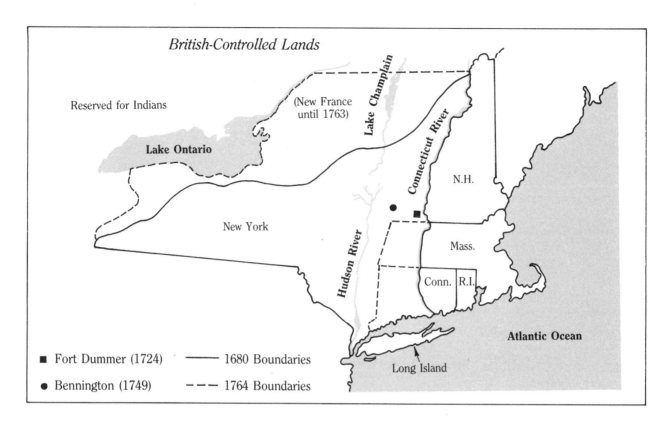

British-Controlled Lands

Reserved for Indians

(New France until 1763)

Lake Champlain

Connecticut River

Lake Ontario

New York

N.H.

Hudson River

Mass.

Conn. | R.I.

Atlantic Ocean

Long Island

■ Fort Dummer (1724)   —— 1680 Boundaries

● Bennington (1749)   - - - 1764 Boundaries

Wentworth ignored the complaint and continued selling land grants. He also had some evidence on his side. In 1724, the colony of Massachusetts had built Fort Dummer on the west side of the Connecticut River. At that time, New Hampshire had complained to the king that it was in their territory. King George had agreed with New Hampshire. The ownership of the land between the Connecticut River and Lake Champlain was indeed in doubt.

Many people said that Wentworth knew he did not own the land as far west as Bennington and was just trying to add to his wealth. But looking at the above map, you will notice that the borders of Massachusetts and Connecticut had moved westward over the years. Perhaps Wentworth believed that his border had moved westward also to become even with theirs. Or perhaps he thought that New York had lost interest in the land and he could add to his colony by claiming it. Whatever the truth of this complicated matter, the turmoil over this "land in between" would last for forty years and cause many hardships for its new inhabitants.

The Grants

When King George received letters from Colden and Wentworth, he ordered that no more land be sold until his decision was made. Wentworth ignored this order and sold 138 townships over the next fifteen years. He sold township grants to rich men who divided the land into smaller "pitches." They then resold the pitches to the men and women who would settle the land. The "land in between" soon became known simply as the Grants.

The earliest settlers came to the Grants in 1761 to establish the towns of Bennington, Guilford, Halifax, Newbury, Pawlet, and Townshend. They used dugout canoes when they could, but mostly they carried their belongings on their backs. The charters for their towns provided for town meetings, fairs, and marketplaces and set aside land for churches and schools.

Most of the new settlers were English people from lower New England who had lived in America for a while. The largest group of non-English settlers was from Scotland. They were the first people to come to Vermont directly after their transatlantic crossing. Because of poverty, crop failures, and few jobs in Britain, many Scottish people were looking for a better life in America.

In 1773, two Scottish men were sent to America to find suitable farmland for a large group of Scots. After scouting the colonies for some time, they decided on the town of Ryegate in Vermont. The first Scottish settlers arrived there in 1774. More followed in 1775 and settled in Barnet. That northeastern county of Vermont became known as Caledonia, the Roman word for Scotland.

While settlers were streaming into the Grants, clearing the land, building homes, and planting crops, the problems between New York and New Hampshire continued. You will recall from Unit 2 that New York was settled after the fashion of the Dutch patroons. Rich men bought a grant from the governor and rented pitches to the people who settled them. Rents were paid to the landowners and their descendants. A portion of these rents went to the king, increasing his wealth. Settlers could never hope to own the land. They had no town meetings and no say in how they were governed.

Note

"Republican" means that the citizens have equality in government. They do not submit to nobility.

In his letters to the king, Colden emphasized these points. He warned that New England governments were "founded on republican principles. . . in opposition to the principles of the Constitution of Great Britain." He urged the king to do something to stop the spread of such dangerous ideas.

The king agreed with Colden, and in 1764, the king's order in council decreed that the Grants belonged to New York. Over the next seventeen years, New York granted two million acres to landlords who rented the land to tenants. Much of this land was already settled by people who had bought it from New Hampshire. Instead of leaving these people alone, New York demanded that the settlers surrender their land titles. They said that the land now belonged to New York and that the settlers who had cleared the land and lived freely for years must rebuy the titles if they wanted to stay. The settlers were furious and angrily refused to pay.

The New York landowners were outraged. The land was legally theirs—how could these farmers refuse to obey the king's orders? They demanded that these upstarts be ejected from the land. The governor sent sheriffs to oust them from their homes. Bands of armed Grantsmen met them and defiantly refused to leave. The sheriffs and other New York officials did not use force on their fellow countrymen and returned home.

The New Yorkers decided to use the courts. They hired James "Swivel Eye" Duane to be their lawyer. He owned much land in New York and the Grants, and he had a reputation as an oppressor of the poor. He was very good at getting what he wanted and filed eviction suits in the New York courts.

Note

An oppressor is someone who cruelly controls someone else. "To evict" means to force or put out.

The Grantsmen knew they were in trouble and looked around for someone who could argue their case against "Swivel Eye" Duane. A young man named Ethan Allen had been spending a lot of time in Arlington visiting his cousin, Remember Baker. He came from northern Massachusetts to hunt, trap, and socialize with the men there. He was an intelligent man who had planned to attend college at Yale before his father died. With his father gone, however, he needed to stay home and help support his

James "Swivel Eye" Duane, lawyer for the New York side of the Grants controversy (Special Collections University of Vermont Library)

Ethan Allen (Courtesy Vermont Historical Society)

family. He never stopped studying, though, and had a real flare for words. The people of the Grants (under the leadership of Seth Warner) asked Ethan to take charge of their case, and he agreed. He was a firm believer in freedom and in the idea that the work of a man's hands belonged to him*—not to a landlord. Besides, he loved a good fight.

Building the State

Much of Vermont's history for the next decade is interwoven with the lives of Ethan Allen, his brother Ira, and their friends. Ethan went right to work to prepare for the court fight against New York. He rode hundreds of miles collecting Wentworth titles and other evidence that would be needed in court. He persuaded Jared Ingersoll to be the lawyer for the Grants. In 1770, Allen and Ingersoll traveled hopefully to the courthouse in Albany, New York. When they tried to present their evidence, however, the judge would not allow the Wentworth titles as evidence. He said that the New Hampshire governor had no right to grant land that belonged to New York (although the titles were made before the king's decision). Allen and Ingersoll were outraged at the judge's one-sidedness. They walked out of the court in protest.

Note

Until his death, Duane insisted that Allen took the money.

Before returning to the Grants, the two stopped at the Albany Tavern for food and drinks. "Swivel Eye" Duane came in and offered Allen money to persuade the Grantsmen to accept New York authority. Allen refused the bribe, using the now-famous words, "The gods of the hills are not the gods of the valleys."

The Green Mountain Boys

Ethan Allen returned to Bennington and met with Seth Warner and Remember Baker at Fay's Tavern. The word spread quickly, and soon two hundred angry men gathered at the tavern. They decided to band together to see that justice was done. They vowed to drive the Yorkers out of the Grants and called themselves the Green Mountain Boys

---

*Women in Vermont were not allowed to own anything—not even the clothes on their backs—until 1779.

The Green Mountain Boys gave opponents the "high chair" treatment as a warning. (Courtesy of National Life Insurance Company, Montpelier, Vermont)

(Yorkers called them the Bennington Mob).* The men elected Allen as their colonel commandant. He ordered harassment and humiliation of all kinds to be used against New York settlers and sympathizers, but he forbade killing anyone. Their work was confined to the western side of the Green Mountains, since the easterners tended to be more conservative and richer and generally accepted Yorker authority.

New York settlers had much to fear from the Green Mountain Boys. Many unsuspecting renters were roughed up and thrown off the land as soon as they arrived. The Green Mountain Boys often attacked at night, their faces blackened with soot. They crept up to newly built fences, cut them, and ran off the cattle. If the renters had already settled in, the Green Mountain Boys destroyed their crops and burned their houses and barns.

Going to town was dangerous if you sympathized with the Yorkers. You could be treated to the "high chair" for several hours or be given the "Beech Seal," in which the backsides of Yorker sympathizers were lashed with a switch from a beech tree. New York surveyors were arrested and given the same kind of treatment. This type of activity went on for two years.

Finally, weary of the harassment, the New York governor offered a compromise.

*Notice how differently language is used depending on your point of view.

If the towns with Wentworth titles paid one-half the value of their property to him, they would own the land free and clear. Some people who could afford it thought this was a reasonable and peaceful way to settle the problem, and ninety-two towns applied to pay the fee.

The Green Mountain Boys, however, were against any payment to New York. The people on the Grants had paid once for their land; why should they pay again? Besides, the leaders owned a lot of land in the Grants by now and could not afford to pay. The Green Mountain Boys rode to the towns that wanted to pay to "convince" them not to. They burned houses, arrested people, lashed them, and threw some off their land, with no chance of collecting their belongings.

Westminster Massacre

Meanwhile, on the eastern side of the Grants, many towns bought titles from New York. Courts run by New York were set up to make sure everyone paid for his land. If one could not afford to pay, the family was thrown off its farm.

On March 13, 1775, the court in Westminster was to open for business. A group of poor farmers met at the courthouse to keep it from opening. It was unusual behavior for law-abiding east-siders, but they were afraid of losing their homes. About a hundred farmers armed with clubs took over the courthouse. The Yorker officials were armed with guns and attacked the farmers. In the riot that erupted, two Grantsmen were shot and killed. That event has been known ever since as the Westminster Massacre.

For the first time, the east-siders felt that they had a serious problem with the Yorkers. The stunned and angry farmers asked the Green Mountain Boys to help them. The east and the west now had one cause and were united in their fight against the government of New York.

During the Revolution

Soon after the "massacre," the Revolutionary War broke out. The Green Mountain Boys rallied behind the rebels and waged one of the first battles of the war. Ethan Allen and Seth Warner met in a tavern in Castleton and planned a raid on Fort Ticonderoga. On the evening of May 10, 1775, eighty-two of the boys sneaked across Lake Champlain under cover of darkness. It took only ten minutes to capture the fort from fewer than fifty startled British soldiers.

This short battle was very important to the rebel cause because of the arms captured at the fort. During the next winter, General George Washington needed the cannons and other arms in Boston, three hundred miles away. A group of rebels brought the weapons by sled and boat, through mud, snow, and freezing temperatures, to General Washington's headquarters. It took forty-eight days, but it was well worth the time and hardships. In March 1776, the rebels attacked Boston. Using the captured cannons, the American army was able to defeat the British and force them to leave Boston. The British were defeated with their own weapons!

Vermont troops went on to fight in several Revolutionary War battles. A Green Mountain Regiment was formed, with the permission of the Continental Congress, to attack the British in Canada. Vermont soldiers met in Dorset to elect a leader; they chose Seth Warner. Ethan Allen was stunned, but people had come to believe that he was a little too hotheaded to be their military leader. This turned out to be true.

Allen was sent to Canada as a civilian to recruit Frenchmen for the Green Mountain Regiment. He was successful and was returning to the regiment with one hundred ten men when something inspired him to attack Montreal. Maybe it was hotheadedness or wanting to prove himself to the men who had voted against him. They were hopelessly outnumbered and surrendered to the British after a short battle. Allen was taken prisoner and locked in irons aboard a schooner for five weeks. He spent the next three years on various prison ships and in prisons on both sides of the Atlantic. Many people were angry at him for giving away the rebel plans to attack Montreal and were not particularly upset about his imprisonment.

The Green Mountain Regiment and another group of Vermonters, Herrick's Rangers, fought successfully for the rebel cause for many years. In the hills near Hubbardton, Vermont, on July 7, 1777, Colonel Seth Warner's rear guard made a desperate stand against pursuing British forces. They were badly beaten. This was the only battle of the Revolution fought on Vermont soil. The Battle of Bennington, fought to protect ammunition stores there, was actually fought in nearby New York.

The Republic of Vermont

While the war raged on, the problems between New York and the Grants were not forgotten. When the colonies proclaimed their independence from Great Britain in 1776, the Grants asked to be admitted to the Union as the fourteenth state. The Continental Congress refused because of New York's claim to the territory. Angered by the refusal and afraid of losing their land to Yorkers, the people met at Westminster in January 1777 to decide what action to take. "In defiance of New York, New Hampshire, King George and...of all the evil powers of the earth and air," they declared themselves the "separate state of New Connecticut."

In July of that same year, delegates met at Elijah West's tavern in Windsor to write a constitution. At that meeting, they declared themselves the independent republic of Vermont. Ira Allen told the story that news of enemy movements along the western border reached the men as they were going over the final draft of the constitution. Alarmed, many wanted to leave to protect their families. Suddenly, a severe thunderstorm raged in the town, keeping the men indoors. It gave them time to finish their work.

Vermont's constitution was different from any other in America. It was the first to outlaw slavery and establish voting rights for men regardless of income or land ownership. One did, however, have to be a man and a Protestant to cast a vote. (In 1793, all men were given the right to vote. Women waited until 1920 for full voting rights.)

In March 1778, Vermont had its first election under the new constitution. Voters chose Thomas Chittenden as the first governor of the republic. He led Vermont from 1778 until he died in 1797, with the exception of one year (1789–1790). Ira Allen was elected treasurer. He was quieter than his brother but wielded much power behind the scenes. These early leaders ruled Vermont firmly for many years.

The Haldimand Affair

In May 1778, Ethan Allen was exchanged for a British officer. He was free at last after

Mrs. Richard Wallace, the wife of an American soldier who swam across Lake Champlain through the enemy fleet to deliver important messages, was a true pioneer woman. She worked her farm in Thetford single-handedly while her husband was with his regiment. (Courtesy of National Life Insurance Company, Montpelier, Vermont)

three years in prison. Returning to Bennington, he was saddened by the news of the deaths of his oldest son, all his brothers (except Ira), and Remember Baker. He rented a house from friends to rest.

Allen learned that even though Vermont was a republic, many people were still interested in joining the United States. They were still nervous about the Yorkers, who continually threatened the republic and repeatedly asked the Continental Congress to help them with their claim.

Allen decided that Vermont needed to pressure the Continental Congress, too. He made three trips to Philadelphia to dicker for recognition of Vermont. He failed each time. He became increasingly pessimistic about Vermont's chances as a free state. The Allens and other leaders of Vermont had more to lose than power if New York won the battle. Over the years, they had become wealthy landowners. They had bought hundreds of acres and thrown off the original inhabitants—the Native Americans. They were becoming desperate; they could accept any government except that of New York. Ethan and Ira Allen looked northward to the British in Canada for help.

By 1780, the Allens began secret talks with the governor of the Province of Quebec, Sir Frederick Haldimand. Ira trekked back and forth between Arlington and Canada to discuss the possibility of Vermont's rejoining the British. The Allens wrote later that these discussions were just a ploy to keep the British from invading Vermont. This

Note

"Pessimistic" means ex-pecting the worst.

may have been true at first, but by the "late spring of 1781, the Arlington conspirators, with Ethan obviously in charge, were hell-bent for treason."*

Rumors of these secret talks soon reached the Vermont assembly. In the past, assembly members had been only too willing to follow the lead of the Allens. Now they became suspicious. The assembly questioned Ira concerning these treasonous talks with Haldimand. He insisted he was only trying to hold off the huge British force in Canada from attacking Vermont. (In reality, Haldimand had only enough men for sporadic raids into Vermont.) The assembly seemed satisfied for the moment.

Note

"Sporadic" means from time to time.

By 1781, Haldimand was ready to announce Vermont's rejoining the British Empire. One event, however, quickly changed the plan. The British Army surrendered at Yorktown, ending the Revolution and the Allens' dream. Through no fault of the Allens, Vermont remained an independent republic for ten more years.

Statehood

After the war, problems flared up occasionally with the Yorkers. The last battle of Ethan Allen and the Green Mountain Boys was in Brattleboro in 1782, where Yorker sympathizers were interfering with the local sheriff. The Green Mountain Boys arrested them, seized their property, and banished them from Vermont. By then, Allen's men had lost a great deal of respect because of the Haldimand talks. When riding through Guilford, citizens fired on the Green Mountain Boys. It was time to call it quits.

Note

Fanny Allen Hospital in Winooski is named after their daughter.

In the meantime, Ethan Allen's first wife had died, and he was remarried in 1784 to a woman named Frances Buchanan, or Fanny. They had three children and later moved to Burlington. Allen died there in the winter of 1789, never seeing the land for which he had given so much become a state.

New people moved to Vermont, and new leaders began taking charge. Businesses were thriving, and farming was good. The first marble quarry in the United States opened in 1785 near Dorset. Vermont even minted its own money in East Rupert. The state was growing up.

In 1787, the Constitutional Congress met to write the U.S. Constitution. Vermonters again asked to be admitted to the Union, but their request was denied because of New York's claim. Spurred on by a stubborn Yankee streak, our forebears continued to seek statehood. By 1789, Kentucky also wanted to join the Union, and the northern states were afraid of being outnumbered by the southern states. New York reluctantly accepted thirty thousand dollars from Vermont to cease its claim. Finally, in 1791, after many years of struggle, Vermont joined the Union as the fourteenth state.

Activity

> *Philosophy*
> (2, 6, 11, 17, 19)
>
> Philosophy is the search for truth and general principles concerning how people should conduct their lives. The writings of an English philosopher named John Locke were very popular with Ethan Allen and other leaders of the Grants. On the next page is a paraphrased idea from *Two Treatises of Government* by Locke. Read it carefully.

*Charles A. Jellison, *Ethan Allen: Frontier Rebel* (Syracuse, N.Y.: Syracuse University Press, 1983), p. 248.

Every man has a property in his own person. The labor of his body and the work of his hands are his. Whatever he removes out of nature, and mixes with his labor, becomes his property.

1. How could Ethan Allen and other Grantsmen use this argument against the Yorkers?
2. Do you agree or disagree with the Allen stand that you imagined in question 1? You must take into account the fact that what they were doing was illegal. They were going against their king and his law.
3. Can something be legally wrong but morally right, or vice versa? Think of some examples. Is it okay to disobey a law that you believe is unjust? Think of some groups besides the Green Mountain Boys that have done this.
4. Should people be punished for disobeying laws they believe are unjust? Such disobedience is called "civil disobedience." Can punishment help their cause? What if we do not punish people who break the law? How do we build respect for the law?
5. Reread John Locke's idea on property. Pretend that you are an Abenaki fighting to save the land of your ancestors. Could you use this argument against the Allens and other whites who say you have no legal right to the land? How do you think Ethan Allen would respond? Have a mock courtroom battle to decide who has the right to the Vermont land.

Activity

A Folk Art Activity
(18)

Everything in Vermont's early days was not seriousness and politics. Plenty of folks were busy trying to make their homes livable and attractive. Today, many of their household decorations are called folk art. These were personal pieces of art created out of materials at hand to be appreciated by family and friends, not sold. Skills for making these items were handed down from generation to generation.

Quilling was one type of folk art used in colonial days. It is an ancient craft that uses basic shapes to form designs, pictures, or messages. Try your hand at it using these directions:

1. Roll thin slips of paper into the basic shapes below. Make up some of your own shapes. Newspaper, wrapping paper, or other thin paper is suitable.

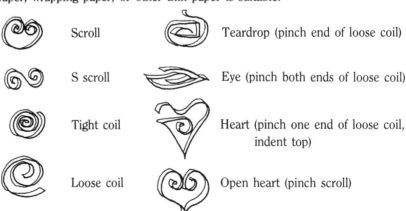

Scroll

S scroll

Tight coil

Loose coil

Teardrop (pinch end of loose coil)

Eye (pinch both ends of loose coil)

Heart (pinch one end of loose coil, indent top)

Open heart (pinch scroll)

V scroll (crease center of paper,
then roll around pencil)*

2. Make pictures or designs that are pleasing to you. Example:

3. Every human being is capable of and needs to express creativity. Create something that is useful and also beautiful for yourself, a member of your family, or a friend. By using only materials at hand, you can be a modern-day folk artist.

Recipe

Sugar Bisquits (Biscuits)
(We call them cookies.)

¾ cup light brown sugar
⅔ cup shortening
1 egg, beaten
1½ cups flour
1½ teaspoons pearl ash (use baking powder)
¼ teaspoon salt
1 teaspoon cinnamon
1 teaspoon vanilla
½ cup plums (use raisins)
4 teaspoons milk

1. Cream sugar and shortening; add egg, milk, and vanilla; beat till fluffy.
2. Sift the dry ingredients; stir into sugar mixture and beat.
3. Stir in raisins. Make into small balls; flatten with fork.
4. Place on greased cookie sheet about 3 inches apart. Bake at 375 °F for 12 to 15 minutes.

Game

Kickery

6 or more players—outdoors or indoors

One player is chosen to be IT and hides in a large place while someone counts to 100. Everyone else yells "Coming" at the end of the count and begins to look for IT. When someone finds IT, they both hide together silently. One player after another finds IT until all have found him or her. The last one to find the group becomes the new IT. The last player may call "Give up" and automatically become IT.

*Adapted from "The Art of Quilling Tree Ornaments," *Early American Life*, special Christmas Edition, 1982, pp. 24–25.

Story

The Rose Garden

*See page 55.

Note

Stumpwork is a cloth picture with some of the figures raised by stuffing small pieces of wood behind the fabric.

Fourteen-year-old Elizabeth Prentis walked in the front door of her house, pretending it was for the first time. She'd been in and out many times while the house was being built, but now it was finished. Finally, they were moving in for good—a little behind schedule—but the whole family had made it through the winter and were together on moving day.

Dressed in her blue homespun dress that she had saved for this occasion, Elizabeth walked through each room downstairs memorizing the textures and designs in the house and furnishings. She concentrated on the feeling of the Oriental rugs beneath her feet, the smoothness of the oak furniture in the dining room, and how perfect the pewter looked on the kitchen table. Her heart seemed to be pounding to be let out of its rib cage.

The other children already were running and laughing upstairs with her parents close behind. Elizabeth didn't want this moment to end. After examining the stumpwork* on the walls, she went outside to the rose garden—anything to prolong this formal introduction to her new home. The warm July sun felt good on her skin as she walked among the bushes covered with small pink blossoms. Their soft scent surrounded her and brought back memories of another time before the house was built.

She vaguely remembered the trip up the Connecticut River in the dugout canoe when she was five. The ox cart piled with their belongings had been lashed to the back of the canoe. Someone drove the oxen along the bank, but she couldn't remember who, as four families had moved together into the Grants. Those four oxen had starved to death that first winter because the thick forest produced no grasses for them to eat.

When she was older and asked her pa why they had moved, he told her that good farmland was cheap and there were no taxes in the Grants. He paid only one shilling an acre for the farmland and could make extra money trapping and contributing to the potash works.*

Since their arrival in Hartford in 1763, the Prentis family had lived in a one-room log cabin. Some land near the cabin had been cleared for farming. Pa also had made a clearing for the big house they were going to build someday when they had enough money. The trees had been used for fuel and potash, and Ma and Pa had planted grass in the clearing. By law every settler had to plant five acres of grass in three years so domesticated animals could live in the wilderness.

Elizabeth remembered one particular day when she and Jeremy had gone to the stream near the clearing for the big house to catch some fish for supper. Pa had been gone for a month delivering potash to Connecticut. Ma was at the cabin sowing some early vegetables.

Suddenly they heard Ma's excited voice coming through the trees. "Hurry, I can't wait to plant them. I know just where I'll put them." Ma hurried into the clearing carrying a big bundle of what look like dead bushes. Pa followed her with more bundles and a digging stick.

"Can't a man even rest after a long journey, Martha?"

"Set them here," she pointed to the post, excitement dancing in her eyes. "I'll take care of everything."

He dropped the burden that he had brought all the way from Connecticut and lay spread-eagled on the grass with an exaggerated sigh. By then, the children had dropped their fishing poles and were running to greet him. "Pa!" Jeremy yelled and jumped onto his chest, hugging him tightly. Elizabeth joined them in the grass, and they rolled and laughed and all talked at the same time about the past month.

By the time they were all talked out, they noticed Ma standing there with tears in her eyes. The sun was fading over the tree tops creating strange shadows around her. Her calico dress, hands, and face were covered with dirt, and the tears overflowed, cleaning little paths down her cheeks. "Now I'm really home, Jason," she said to Pa. "This rose garden is the beginning of our real home."

Elizabeth would never forget that picture of her mother crying and smiling among the crooked shadows of the forest. It was something everyone did a lot of in those first years— smiling and crying.

As that happy memory faded, another darker one took its place. She tried to push this new memory aside, but it was unrelenting, and she soon gave in to it.

She looked back to the winter of 1772 when Pa had gone to a meeting at the MacIntyres. King George had said that the Grants belonged to New York, and this worried people in Hartford because they had bought their land from the governor of New Hampshire. People heard stories about Yorkers on the other side of the mountains trying to throw people off their land. Today Pa and the others were meeting to decide what to do about the problem. He should have been home for dinner, but they had already eaten, cleaned up, and put Jeremy and Kathleen to bed.

Elizabeth glanced at her mother, who was just staring into the fire, her open poetry book on her lap. A wolf howled outside, and Ma jumped involuntarily. "I wish your pa would get home," she said. "I worry about him out in those woods at night."

They sat for a while listening to the mingling howls of the wolves and the wind. Finally Ma got up and put on her cape. She lit a torch in the fire and picked up the rifle. "I'm going to look for your pa. You stay here and look after the children."

Elizabeth did as she was told, shivering every time the wind blew its icy breath between the cracks in the logs. Finally, she heard Ma coming back pulling something on the sled. When she opened the door she saw Pa's crumpled and bleeding body being guided along the path toward the door. Elizabeth thought for sure he was dead and ran out crying into the darkness to help her ma.

"He's not dead." Her mother's voice cracked with despair. "He's been badly mauled by a wolf. Help me get him inside." After they had dragged him to the bed, Ma said, "He must've killed the wolf before he passed out—it's dead back there a ways."

They washed his wounds, and Ma sewed up what she could with her needle and thread. "Get me that moldy bread in the cupboard," she said to Elizabeth. Ma spread the bread over the wounds. "This should keep him from getting all infected," she said.

But Pa did get infected. All they could do was wash him, force some liquids down his throat, and pray. His fever only got worse, and he moaned most of the time, but the Prentis family kept hoping and praying that he would pull through.

When the wood was getting low, Elizabeth hitched up the oxen and went into the forest to chop wood. She drew the timbers closer to the cabin and cut them into firewood. She'd get cold and weak, and her fingers would crack and bleed from the cold, but she kept going because she felt as if she was doing something for Pa.*

After a while, Pa started to get better. Jeremy had brought the wolf skin to town for the twenty-dollar bounty. It was the first thing he showed Pa when he could sit up. "This'll help us finish up the new house, won't it Pa?"

---

*The information in this paragraph is based on a real happening in Bennington county.

"Sure will, son, but it'll be a little later than we planned, with me laid up all this time."

"Don't worry about that," said Ma. "We can wait a little longer." She smiled for the first time in a month.

A voice summoned Elizabeth back to the present. "Are you coming upstairs to see our room?" Kathleen called from the upstairs window. Elizabeth took a deep breath, inhaling the perfume of the roses. "Coming," she answered.

She was ready to leave the past to see the new bedroom that she would be sharing with Kathleen. Elizabeth knew that from now on the rose garden would be her secret place to get away from everyone and dream.

UNIT 4

Early Roads and Transportation

The first ancient people to arrive on the land now called Vermont used the oldest form of transportation known to humans: walking. Perhaps that is how you arrived at school this morning. At some later point (no one is sure exactly when), the Native Americans discovered that a hollowed-out log, or dugout canoe, worked well on the waterways. These two forms of transportation served Vermonters well for thousands of years.

As the people moved around the state, they gradually beat down paths connecting the waterways. Eventually, Vermont's streams, rivers, and lakes were connected by these paths. One could travel from the Connecticut River up one of its tributaries, carry a canoe to another river (carrying the canoe is known as a portage), and travel down it until reaching Lake Champlain. The first Europeans to set eyes on Vermont used the same land and water routes of the Native Americans.

Soon, however, the ancient paths could not accommodate the thousands of Europeans and their belongings. By the end of the eighteenth century, more than eighty-six thousand whites had made homes here. The old paths were not wide enough for their wagons and often did not extend to where the whites owned land. Farms needed to be connected to the towns that were springing up. This unit will explore the transportation changes that moved through Vermont in the eighteenth century.

Note

A tributary is a stream or river that flows into a larger one.

Moving Around Vermont

Many of the first white families moving to Vermont used dugout canoes to carry their belongings. Others walked the frozen rivers in the winter or used the ancient paths, carrying what they could on their backs. It was said that if you could not carry one hundred pounds for ten miles, you were not fit to settle in Vermont.

Beasts of burden were pretty useless. There were no grasses to feed the animals, and those that were used soon died of starvation. Even if there was feed, they could not have pulled a wagon or an ox cart—the paths were not wide enough. With time, both these problems were solved. A law was passed that required every settler to plant five acres of grass within three years, and the forest paths were widened enough to accommodate wagons. Animals could then be used to help ease the difficulties of moving into the wilderness.

Still, it was no picnic traveling on these paths. They were muddy in the spring and full of bumps and ruts in the summer and fall. It was easier gliding along snow-packed paths or frozen streams in the winter. Sleighs became a popular form of transportation.

But the settlers could not limit travel to the winter months. Road building became an important chore for the settlers. The first road built through the state was a military road from Fort #4 in Charlestown, New Hampshire, to Chimney Point in Vermont. It was completed in 1760, and markers point out the old route in several towns today.

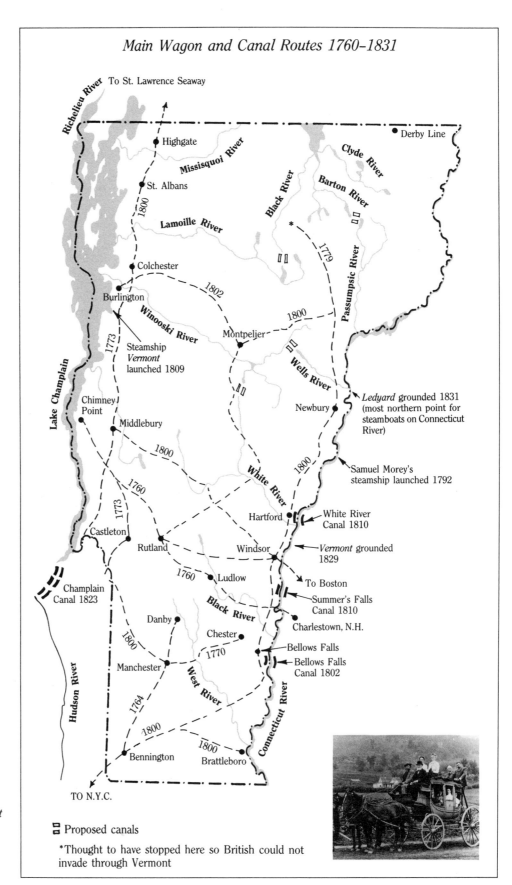

Main Wagon and Canal Routes 1760–1831

To St. Lawrence Seaway

Richelieu River

Highgate

Derby Line

Missisquoi River

Clyde River

St. Albans

Black River

Barton River

Lamoille River

1800

Passumpsic River

Colchester

*

1802

1779

Burlington

Winooski River

1800

Montpelier

Steamship
Vermont
launched 1809

1773

Wells River

Lake Champlain

Chimney
Point

Newbury

Ledyard grounded 1831
(most northern point for
steamboats on Connecticut
River)

Middlebury

1800

1800

White River

Samuel Morey's
steamship launched 1792

1760

1773

Hartford

White River
Canal 1810

Castleton

Windsor

Vermont grounded
1829

Rutland

To Boston

1760   Ludlow

Summer's Falls
Canal 1810

Champlain
Canal 1823

Danby

Black River

Charlestown, N.H.

Chester

Bellows Falls

1770

Bellows Falls
Canal 1802

Hudson River

Manchester

West River

1764

1800

Connecticut River

1800

1800

Bennington   Brattleboro

TO N.Y.C.

▯ Proposed canals

*Thought to have stopped here so British could not
invade through Vermont

As towns sprouted up, more roads were needed to connect farm to town and one town to another. Lotteries sometimes were used to raise money for the roads. It became the responsibility of every man from sixteen to sixty (except ministers, college professors, and college students) to work on the roads for four days every year. They were not always happy about it, but they tried to keep the roads in good condition.

Between 1795 and 1810, Vermont experienced a great flurry of road-building activity. Private turnpike companies sprang up to improve the primitive roads. To make money doing this, they set up tollgates, where travelers paid for using the road. (This was not a new idea, as the Persians had first used toll roads about four thousand years ago.) By the 1800s, public highways ran from north to south and connected the Connecticut and Champlain valleys.

Tolls were very unpopular, however, as you can imagine, and the price of travel on these roads was very expensive. In 1815, it cost $2.75 for one wagon with one passenger to ride from Bennington to Brattleboro. Few people could afford such outrageous prices, and they made paths around the tolls to avoid paying the fares. Companies soon found it difficult to make a profit at the tolls. By the 1850s, they had turned over maintenance of the roads to the towns.

Types of Roads

The first dirt roads were made by scraping paths along the forest floor. Later, corduroy, plank, and macadam roads were built. Corduroy roads were made by laying logs across the wetlands. The log trail looked like corduroy material. Horses got their legs caught between the logs, however, and that idea was abandoned.

A cheaper, safer road was a plank road. One or two tracks of planks, about four yards wide, were laid for wagons. Many a farm was connected to town by these roads. Later, these roads connected farms to the railroad lines so farmers could easily transport their goods. Planks rot, however, after sitting out in the snow, rain, and mud. It became too much work to repair these roads, and in time, plank roads also were abandoned.

Macadam (crushed and packed stone) came into use during the nineteenth century. This road was named after MacAdam, its Scottish inventor, and is still used occasionally today, especially for driveways. Can you think of the advantage that macadam had over dirt or wood?

Stagecoaches

With the coming of statehood, more and more people began flowing into Vermont. Road improvements paved the way for a new type of transportation to carry them to the Green Mountains. By the beginning of the 1800s, stages were winding their way through the state. They were called stagecoaches because trips were done in "stages" to change horses and to give weary passengers a rest.

These trips were at best unenjoyable and at worst grueling and hazardous. Imagine that you need to go from Burlington to Windsor—a distance of about one hundred miles. You are jammed into the coach with five other people. Two men are smoking cigars; a child is crying on her mother's lap. As you travel along the road, depending on the season, dust, rain, or snow spits at you through the windows. You bump along for a while, wishing the seat was a little softer, when suddenly the stage gives a wild jolt and stops. It is stuck in a rut. You must get out and help free the heavy vehicle from the furrow. Back on the road again, your coach comes to a steep hill. You must get out once more and help push it up to the top. When going down hills, the driver chains the wheels to keep the stage from speeding out of control. Again, you must walk. Due to the poor condition of the road, you may be delayed further, forced to wait outside in the heat (or rain or snow) while a broken axle is fixed.

At the next stop, a very well-dressed man and woman are waiting with their bags. The driver asks you and another not-so-well-dressed passenger to sit on top with the baggage to make room for them. You continue your trip even more uncomfortable than before. When evening comes, you are happy to see the lights of the inn burning in the distance.

After dinner, dreaming of a comfortable night's sleep, you climb the stairs to your room. Wearily, you settle into bed, only to find it is inhabited by some unknown vermin. You get little sleep as you scratch your way through the night. In the morning, you awake to face another day of traveling toward your destination.

Trips such as this were common in the early days of our state. Wagons, buggies, ox carts, sleighs, and stages were the only means of overland travel until the trains arrived in the mid-nineteenth century. In the next section, we will explore the trains and ships that brought enormous changes to Vermont life. We also will meet the many people who streamed into our state using these forms of transportation.

SECTION II

The Ups and Downs of the 19th Century

UNIT 5

Water and Land Travel

The Chinese say that sails are like the human ear, always listening for the wind. For centuries, people depended on the wind to billow their sails and carry them across the sea. Many of the important inventions concerning sailing vessels originated in China while "the Europeans were still coasting in cockleshells."*

Gradually, the Europeans learned many things about sailing from the Arabs, who had learned it from the Chinese. Soon the white people were starting out on their own across the huge, unknown waters of the earth, as other races had before them. It is hard to say what the history of the world would have been like if people had not sailed away from their homelands in search of adventure, new items to trade, and new places to live.

Traveling in wooden sailing vessels was *the* way to travel until the nineteenth century. It was slow and could take months to cross the ocean. It also was very dangerous; many a traveler never made it home. Then Americans came up with a major invention—probably the first American invention to affect history so profoundly. We gave the world the steamboat. This invention, along with the railroad, caused enormous changes to take place in nineteenth-century Vermont. We will study both of these in this unit.

Steamboats

The idea that led to the steamboat—that is, using steam power—had been around for a long time. In 1765, a Scotsman named James Watt finally invented a steam engine. People became excited about all the possible ways to use it. One idea that many inventors sweated over was using it to turn a huge paddle wheel to power a boat.

In 1792, a Vermont pioneer in steam navigation launched a steamboat on the Connecticut River near Fairlee. His name was Sam Morey (refer back to map on page 42). He shared his ideas with Robert Fulton, who had promised to pay him for the ideas and models. Fifteen years later, Fulton launched the *Claremont*, usually considered the first successful steamboat. Morey never received the money Fulton promised him and angrily accused Fulton of stealing his idea. Morey did not have a patent, however, so Fulton is credited with the invention in most history books.

The next U.S. steamboat, called the *Vermont*, was launched at Shelburne in 1809. The steamboat era had begun, and Vermonters took advantage of this new form of transportation to help their businesses. They knew they could use this quicker form of transportation to get their goods to markets in big cities, but something else was needed first: canals.

The first canal in the state was built on the Connecticut River in 1802. Finally,

*Alan Villiers, *Men, Ships and the Sea* (Washington, D.C.: National Geographic Society, 1962), p. 57.

boats could get by Bellows Falls safely and quickly. Two more canals followed farther north, and steamboats attempted to navigate the waters of the river. It proved to be a rather difficult task, and several ships grounded in the shallows.

On the western side of the state, the Champlain Canal between Waterford, New York, and Whitehall, New York, was completed in 1823. The canal connected Lake Champlain to New York City via the Hudson River. Western Vermonters finally had a water connection to a big American city. Instead of depending solely on Canadian customers, many Vermonters could now sell their goods to the south. Vermont's wooden products, farm produce, and minerals began floating southward to big American markets.

Freight and passengers were carried through the canal on flat-bottom boats called packets. They were slowly pulled along by mules or horses. Packets had cabins with one long table, a stove, and rows of bunks. Often people who did not get a bunk drew lots to see who would use the table as a bed. People did not mind the discomfort too much; it was a much cheaper and faster way to travel than by ox cart or stagecoach. And a more comfortable steamship was waiting at the other end of the canal.

A new kind of fever raged in the Green Mountains: canal fever. Plans were made all over the state to connect the waterways with canals. But before most of the digging had begun, something new that would doom the steamship industry came chugging and smoking into sight. The "iron horse," or railroad, had come to Vermont.

The railroad did not, however, affect ocean travel. Until the 1850s, the immigrants coming into Vermont had crossed the ocean in sailing vessels. The trip took anywhere from six weeks to three months depending on the weather. Those too poor to buy a regular ticket (as were most of the travelers) bought a ticket for the steerage compartment. It was in the bottom of the ship near the steering equipment. Sailing companies put as many people down there as would fit. It was airless and dark, and it smelled terrible after a few days at sea. It was an unhealthy way to spend a few months, and many people did not live through the voyage.

By the late nineteenth century, most shipping companies had changed to steamships. Poorer customers still had to travel in steerage, but travel time was cut to as little as ten days. A ticket was a lot cheaper for these shorter trips, and this helped convince many people to come to America. It seemed as if the floodgates had opened as people came steaming across the ocean.

First Stop in America

The states along the East Coast that had ports for these transatlantic ships were flooded with immigrants. Landing in a strange country was confusing for the newcomers, especially if they did not speak English. Many dishonest people tried to take advantage of them. Because the immigrants did not understand our culture and usually were uneducated, they became easy prey for swindlers. At first, ethnic organizations tried to protect people from these hucksters, but the job soon became overwhelming.

Some states set up safe places where newcomers could get hospital attention and job information, arrange for a place to stay, and change their money. The biggest place was Castle Garden in New York City. The army even set up recruiting stations there during the Civil War.

With the millions of immigrants coming into our country, however, New York could not afford to keep running this refuge without help from the federal (national) government. The state needed money to hire more workers because people were still being swindled. In 1882, new laws were passed restricting the number and types of immigrants. A new and bigger place was needed to screen them.

Note

Today, Ellis Island is a national park. It is being restored in preparation for its one-hundredth birthday in 1992.

The federal government set up an immense new complex on Ellis Island in New York Harbor (near Liberty Island, which holds the Statue of Liberty). It opened in 1892, and all immigrants to the East Coast had to pass through its halls. If your ancestors came to the East Coast between 1892 and 1943, they landed first on Ellis Island.

The people working there checked the immigrants' health and legal right to come to America. The United States' new laws frightened many newcomers; they were afraid they might be sent back home without having a chance to live their dreams. Here are some of the laws. What do you think of them? People with certain diseases (such as tuberculosis and glaucoma) were not allowed to enter the United States. Convicts and lunatics were sent back to their homeland. Starting in 1882, people from China were not allowed in. Later, the number of Japanese allowed to enter the country was restricted. By the early twentieth century, those who could not read were rejected, and many more people were refused entry because of their nationality.

The island became known as the Island of Tears because some people were told that they could not settle in America. After a short examination, twenty percent of the newcomers were sent back to the ships to return home or were held for further questioning. Many people's hopes were dashed without ever setting foot on mainland America.

The majority, however, were allowed to continue their journey to New York City or to other places in the country. Thousands came to Vermont to find jobs. Instead of getting into ox carts or stagecoaches, as they had at the beginning of the century, they now had new choices. They could travel by steamship or railroad.

The Railroad Industry

Note

A famine is a severe food shortage causing great hunger.

Even before the railroads began carrying immigrants into Vermont, the railroad industry brought people here for jobs. Building the railroad was a difficult and dangerous job, one that the old established immigrants did not want to do. People fleeing famine, unemployment, or cruel governments across the sea would do just about anything to make a living, so many new immigrants came to Vermont to build our railroads.

The railroad companies built shanties (shacks) for the workers to live in along the tracks. They also provided food. By the time these expenses were taken out of their pay, the workers earned about four cents an hour. Peddlers followed the construction gangs to sell them needed items and relieve them of that small amount of money. It was not an easy life.

Many dangers were involved in building the railroads. Men occasionally were blown up in blasting accidents or cave-ins. Derricks moving loads of lumber or tracks sometimes dropped their loads on workers. Despite these difficulties, immigrants built five hundred miles of tracks throughout the state. Doing so cost many lives and about twenty-six million dollars. The first train to run on these tracks chugged from White River Junction to Montpelier in 1848. The "iron horse" had come to Vermont.

The railroads did not make a great deal of money for either the builders or the owners. But others in the state benefited immensely from the new industry. Companies that had been limping along because they were not located near the waterways could now expand. They could get their goods to city markets quickly and cheaply. The lumber and quarrying industries exploded with activity. Slate production alone increased by five hundred percent. Farm values near the lines rose because it cost farmers less to

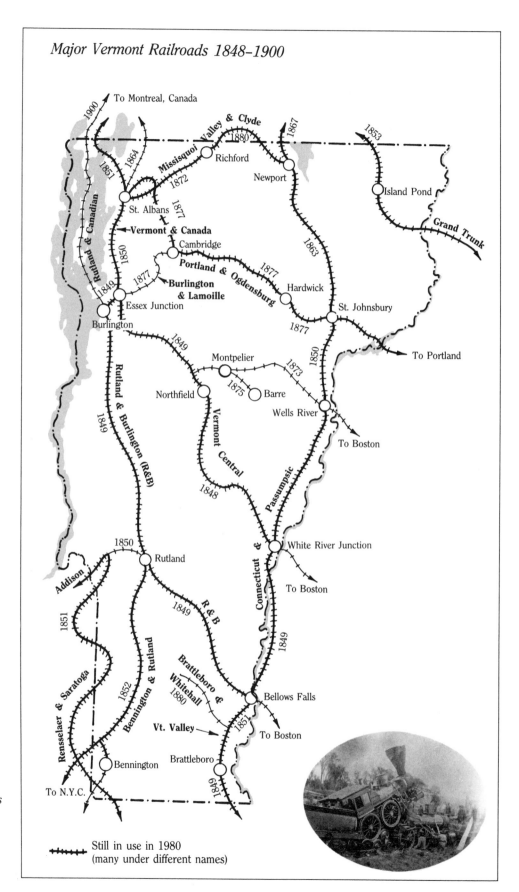

Major Vermont Railroads 1848–1900

To Montreal, Canada

1900

1864

1851

Rutland & Canadian

1850

1849

St. Albans

1877

Vermont & Canada

1877

Burlington & Lamoille

Essex Junction

Burlington

1849

Missisquoi Valley & Clyde

1880

Richford

1872

Newport

1867

1853

Island Pond

Grand Trunk

Cambridge

Portland & Ogdensburg

1877

Hardwick

1863

St. Johnsbury

1877

To Portland

1849

Montpelier

1873

1850

Northfield

1875

Barre

Wells River

To Boston

Rutland & Burlington (R&B)

1849

Vermont Central

1848

Passumpsic

Connecticut &

White River Junction

1850

Rutland

1849

R & B

To Boston

Addison

1851

Rensselaer & Saratoga

1852

Bennington & Rutland

Brattleboro & Whitehall

1880

Vt. Valley

1849

Bellows Falls

1851

To Boston

Bennington

Brattleboro

1849

To N.Y.C.

Still in use in 1980
(many under different names)

MISSISQUOI SPRINGS HOTEL.

This Hotel is adjacent to the famous Missisquoi Springs, in

FRANKLIN CO., VERMONT,

IS FIRST CLASS IN EVERY RESPECT,

and delightfully located, where the pure dry Vermont air will be found very invigorating, and the SCENERY WILD AND PICTURESQUE, with fine views of MOUNT MANSFIELD AND THE ADIRONDACKS.

(Special Collections University of Vermont Library)

get their products to market. Cattle prices were better because the cattle did not lose weight on a long overland foot journey to market.

New hotels, restaurants, and stores were needed along the lines for workers and passengers. The rails not only carried people *into* our state, but they also carried people out. Job seekers went south and west to start new lives in other parts of the country.

The railroads helped attract a new kind of traveler called a tourist. Many wealthy people in the big cities wanted to get away from their hot, dusty, crowded streets in the summer. With the coming of the railroad, a trip into the cool, quiet Green Mountains became easier.

Tourism began slowly. Vermonters were not always happy to see people who did nothing but relax and wear fancy clothes come into their communities. But they soon learned there was money to be made from them. Houses were built on the mountain peaks to attract city folks to the healthy mountain air. Hotels grew up near the state's many mineral springs, which were said to have the power to cure a number of illnesses. (There is no medical evidence for this.)

The most successful springs were those near the railroad lines. Large resorts sprang up in Clarendon, Guilford, Highgate, Middletown, and Sheldon. Sheldon had seven hotels at one time and offered horseback riding, lawn bowling, croquet, and bottled water to take back to the city. Although the springs mania did not last long, Vermont's tourist industry was launched thanks to the rails of the iron horse.

Riding these rails was not always safe or comfortable. Derailings and collisions with animals and people on the tracks caused many accidents. Wheels came off, and boilers sometimes exploded. Crossing a bridge was particularly dangerous. Freezing, thawing, and flooding weakened the wooden structures, and the weight of the train caused some bridges to collapse. Sparks from the train also set bridges on fire. Loss of life and limb was not uncommon.

Railroad management was poor in the early days. Everything was so new that no one had experience with scheduling or making customers comfortable. Competing lines did not work well together, and connections were terrible. To attract passengers, some lines offered free or reduced fares. With time, many problems were solved. People saw what a shot in the arm the trains were to Vermont and accepted them as an important part of its changing scenery.

Transportation improvements and inventions had brought Vermont closer to the rest of the country. For better or for worse, it was no longer isolated. New people with new ideas came streaming into the state, setting up farms, cutting down the forests, and building new industries. In the next two units, we will meet those people who came to Vermont along our roadways and waterways seeking new opportunities in the Green Mountains.

Activity

*A Railroad Song**
(17, 18)

Read over the old song reprinted here. Learn how to sing it. What does the "Hartford Wreck" tell you about the safety of the early railroads? How do you think little Joe McGret feels about riding the rails? Write a poem about Joe's feelings or about your own feelings.

Hartford Wreck

'Twas the Mon-tre-al Ex-press It was

speed-ing at its best, When near the Hart-ford bridge it

struck a bro-ken rail. And with a fear-ful

crash To the riv-er bed it dashed, And

few sur-vived to tell that aw-ful tale.

In some country far or near
Each day we used to hear
Of some accident on land or sea,
Your attention now I'll call
To the latest of them all
'Tis the Central Vermont tragedy.

It was in the dead of night
And no words could paint that sight
The sleeping cars were filled with living
  freight
When with a fearful crash
To the river bed it dashed
And few survived to tell that awful tale.

It was shocking to relate
And sad to contemplate.
No words can paint a picture of that sight
Little they thought that death was nigh
When they bid their friends good-bye
When leaving home upon that fatal night.

'Twas the Montreal Express
It was speeding at its best
When near the Hartford bridge it struck
  a broken rail
And with a fearful crash
To the river bed it dashed
And few survived to tell that awful tale.

Soon the wreck was all ablaze
There amid the victims gazed
The piercing cries for help was sad to hear
None responded to their call
They must perish one and all
Alas, kind friends no help for them was near.

There is one we ne'er forget
It was little Joe McGret
Who was with his father on that fatal train
And though wounded by the fall
When he heard his father's call
To free him from the wreck he tried in vain.

"It's no use, my boy," said he,
"There's no help for you or me."
Just then, the flames around them curled
Little Joe began to cry
When his father said "good-bye
We meet again but in another world."

*From *A Vermont Songbook* reprinted with the permission of the Vermont Historical Society.

UNIT 6

The Rhythms of Nature

Huge amounts of unsettled land attracted thousands of people to Vermont to farm at the turn of the century. Because of better roads and vehicles, people came pouring across the borders like water through a bursting dam. By 1800, the population had jumped from 86,000 at statehood to more than 154,000. Within another ten years, it had climbed to 218,000. Vermont was the fastest growing state in the Union.

Who were these people? Why did they come? Briefly, they came seeking land and new opportunities in a state that offered various ways of earning a living. Most newcomers farmed in the early part of the century. Later they worked in the industries that sprouted in the cities (see Unit 7). They came from other states and other countries on foot and by sail, steamboat, stagecoach, train, and wagon—any way they could manage.

Note

Population is not just people moving in and out but also births and deaths.

Then, almost as soon as it had begun, Vermont's population explosion stopped. Some people had made their dreams come true in Vermont, but by the mid-1800s, two out of every five people were leaving. Vermont became the slowest growing state in the Union as people moved to other New England cities or to the beckoning West. Those leaving were replaced by thousands of immigrants flowing into Vermont from other countries. The reasons for these comings and goings will be explored in the next two units. First, let's go back to the turn of the century.

Historical Background

Imagine that the year is 1795. You are seventeen years old and living in Salisbury, Connecticut, with your parents and eight brothers and sisters. You feel crowded at home; you never have any privacy. You have been feeling restless and are eager to move out on your own. You have some money saved from working at the general store but not enough. Land is pretty scarce and expensive in Connecticut. Lately you have been courting a girl and are thinking of getting married. But where will you live?

One day, while sweeping out the store, you hear two customers talking about the new state of Vermont. Land is cheap, and forests and game are abundant. A family could make a living selling potash and hunting and trapping while the first year's crops are growing. Sounds like just what you've been dreaming about.

Scenes like this one have been replayed thousands of times since Europeans started pouring into our state. People arrived in the state looking for a plot of land on which to earn a livelihood. They were mostly self-sufficient farmers trying to clear land for crops. Everyone—men, women, and children—worked hard in the battle to subdue nature and eke out a living. It was not as it is today, when we are finally learning that we must work *with* nature to survive. Before the nineteenth century was over, however, Vermonters would learn that lesson—the hard way.

Early Farmers

Note

"To export" means to sell out of state or out of the country.

The first crop these newcomers harvested was the forests. They did not need to plant first; that had been taken care of eons ago by the glacier. They used the ancient trees to build homes, as fuel, and as potash. Potash was a main ingredient in manufacturing bleaches and soaps. It was made by burning wood. Several families worked together to contribute wood ashes to a big iron pot. From these ashes, the settlers made a liquid called lye. When the liquid was boiled away, a gray powder called *potash* was left.

A process for making potash (or pearlash) was perfected by Vermonter Samuel Hopkins in 1790. The first patent signed by President George Washington was for this Pittsford man's discovery. It took about five tons of wood to make thirty-nine pounds of potash. During the 1790s, Vermonters produced and exported hundreds of tons of potash each year. Imagine how many clearings were chopped in the once-lush forests. Many animal species gradually lost their habitat and disappeared from the state.

Despite the changes the industry brought to Vermont, farmers depended on the extra income. They brought the potash to trade at the general store—if there was one—or took it to a bigger city in lower New England, New York, or Quebec. A trip to the city would mean a chance to catch up on the news and buy new clothes, tools, and books that were not found on the Vermont frontier. The potash industry was very important to the social and economic way of life in early Vermont.

In the early 1800s, however, a French scientist discovered that sodium could be used instead of potash in the manufacturing process. Sodium was much easier to acquire, since it was simply dug out of the ground. In a few years, the bottom fell out of Vermont's first great industry. People continued to make potash into the 1850s, but it was not as profitable. This was only the first of many blows to hit Vermont farmers in the years to come.

Wheat

Note

By 1899, there were 1.7 million apple trees in Vermont.

Note

Dust and ash from a volcanic explosion in Tambora, Indonesia, caused the cold that summer. The dust floated around the globe and kept the sun's rays from heating as they should.

Exactly how were farmers using the clearings created by the potash industry? They were planting vegetables, wheat, and fruit trees (apples did best) and raising small numbers of livestock, such as cows, pigs, and sheep. When the weather was good and the crops were healthy, a family lived well on what it produced on the farm. Some years were bad, however, especially 1816. That year was so cold that ice frosted the crops every month in the summer. Crops suffered, and farmers became extremely discouraged.

A family needed some money put away for years like that. The small plots of wheat gradually grew to larger plots. Soon farmers were growing more than they needed and selling the extra for cash. Gristmills sprang up along the many streams to grind the wheat into flour for export. The Vermont soil was still fertile, and families made a decent living.

But gradually, the soil wore out. People had overestimated the fertility of the hills, and by 1820, the farming boom was over. (Remember from Unit 1 that much of the eastern part of our state is underlaid with granite. Granite causes the soil to be too acidic for farming. Due to our highlands, the growing season in many regions is too short.) Thousands of people came to Vermont with dreams, but "guiding a plow across a hillside that is as irregular as a roller coaster, and as full of rocks as a pudding is of plums, is a work for a superoptimist."* The wheat weevil (a type of insect) and wheat rust also helped drive the farmers from the hills. Soon Vermonters were importing flour

*Lewis Stilwell, *Migration From Vermont* (Montpelier, Vermont: Vermont Historical Society, 1948), p. 70.

This woman is shown twisting yarn at a farm. (Courtesy Vermont Historical Society)

from the West instead of exporting it.

Vermont's once-bustling hill towns and farms were losing people in great numbers. Some caught a new fever called "western fever." Farmers began swarming to the wide-open spaces and fertile soil of the West. The completion of the Erie Canal across New York State in 1825 helped travelers on their way. Many people who were not moving west were moving into the cities looking for work. The character of Vermont was changing once again.

Sheepherding

The farmers who stayed started a new revolution in Vermont. They began to specialize in a new breed of animal—merino sheep. Because of their cleft lip, merinos can graze on just about any kind of land, and the rocky Vermont soil was fine for them.

The first merinos were brought to Vermont in 1810 by Colonel William Jarvis of Weathersfield. He was the U.S. consul in Spain when a civil war broke out. Normally, the Spanish guarded their sheep well, not allowing them to leave the country. But the war was creating havoc, and Jarvis was able to smuggle some out of Spain and onto his farm in Vermont.

"Merino mania" took hold in the Green Mountains, and by 1840, there were more than five sheep for every human being in the state. Many farmers were growing rich on wool production, and many others were growing rich processing the wool into cloth (see Unit 7).

You might think that this mania would attract farmers to Vermont, but exactly the opposite happened. Sheep need a lot of room to graze and not many people to take care of them. The more successful farmers bought out others to have more room for grazing. Farms became larger and fewer. This is one reason the farming population began the decline that has continued to today.

By the 1850s, Vermont's economy was on another downslide. Not only were the people migrating to the West, but the sheep were, too! The U.S. government lifted

These merino sheep were raised at the Irving Eastman farm. (Courtesy Vermont Historical Society)

Note

A tariff is a tax put on goods coming into a country.

its protective tariff on sheep, and the price of wool went down. Since farming was cheaper in the West, the plunging prices did not hurt western sheep farmers as much as Vermont farmers. Once again, Vermonters found it difficult to compete with the westerners, and they got out of the business fast, selling their flocks to westerners or even Australians.

People began to panic. What could they do to make a living? Some people tried a very unlikely enterprise: They planted mulberry trees to raise silkworms. Dreams of silk riches danced in their heads. They soon found, however, that Vermont's climate was not as good as China's for silkworms. Something else was needed to fill the gap left by the migrating merinos.

Dairying

Vermonters had always kept a few cows on the farm for their own milk, butter, and cheese. There also were quite a few beef cattle in the state that were sold to markets in the Boston area. Vermonters who decided to try and make a go of it in farming turned to dairy cows and beef cattle in greater numbers.

Like sheep, cows need a lot of room to graze. In fact, the land needed for five sheep was enough for only one cow. The big farms needed to get bigger, and the smaller farmers again were bought out. Dairy farmers needed better land for growing feed, so the retreat from the hill farms continued as farmers searched for fertile land in the valleys. People also continued swarming to the West. By 1860, forty-two percent of the people born in Vermont were living outside the state.

Dairy farming was not an overnight success. Vermont cows were a pretty scrawny lot. Their production of milk remained low until a few improvements were made. In 1869, the first statewide dairy association in the United States was formed in Vermont. Farmers joined together to keep up on the newest techniques. They did not have to look far to find major improvements. In the 1880s, the first silo in the United States was built in Vermont. This was a big improvement, as keeping feed in silos allows it to keep its nutrients longer. Cows were better fed in the winter, and milk production shot up. A better breed of cow began to replace the shabby cow of earlier times.

By the mid-1800s, the railroads had connected Vermont to regional and national markets. Farmers began making an excess of butter and cheese and exporting them to city markets. For decades, women had done most of this type of work on the farm. Cheese factories and creameries soon began dotting the state, however. In 1854, the first cheese factory opened and in 1871, the first creamery. It took a while before farmers were willing to change their ways, but as demand for their products grew, they gradually began to change. By the end of the century, fifty-five percent of Vermont's butter was churned at creameries, and ninety-two percent of its cheese was made at the factory.

The St. Albans butter market became famous nationwide; the Franklin County Creamery was the largest in the world. As you may have guessed, creameries collected milk from thousands of cows and separated the cream from the skim milk. The cream was later sold as sweet cream or churned into butter for export.

The exporting of milk had to await the arrival of refrigerated railroad cars. As this newest form of transportation spread throughout Vermont in the latter half of the nineteenth century, the dairy industry received another boost. Milk could now join butter and cheese as exports. All these products could travel farther under refrigeration. By 1900, Vermont had made another successful transition and was known as a dairy state. Dairying remained its leading industry until the 1940s.

The People Who Built Our Farming Tradition

Even though farming has long and tiresome hours and Mother Nature makes some years very difficult, farmers find living close to nature satisfying. Being outside much of the time and tending to animals creates a closeness with nature that indoor jobs cannot provide. That feeling is similar no matter where on earth you go. Vermonters began to learn this during the nineteenth century.

Most of the farmers who entered Vermont came from other New England states. They were of English descent, white, and Protestant. Although there were many differences among individual men and women, they understood the same basic things. Their language, religion, and customs were the same, and they were comfortable with the way their neighbors viewed the world.

Then, slowly at first, people with different languages and customs began to settle in the Green Mountains. They were searching for the same kind of life that farmers everywhere enjoy. Some of the English people saw these differences as exciting; the newcomers brought new ideas and gave the English residents a chance to learn more about their world. Others were suspicious of the immigrants whom they could not understand and would have nothing to do with them. Treating people unkindly because of their differences (discrimination) caused many problems among the people of Vermont. Unfortunately, it was not the first time people acted cruelly toward their neighbors, and it would not be the last.

Who were these new people—welcomed by some and scorned by others? The early foreign-born farmers were from northern Europe and Canada. They were usually poor people who had been discriminated against in their homeland. Or because of war, famine, or crop failures, they could no longer survive in their native land.

Vermont farming families join together for a barn raising. (Special Collections University of Vermont Library)

"How could poor people afford to travel to a faraway country?" you might ask. The French Canadians, of course, did not have as far to go. They could walk over the border into Vermont. Others, who needed the fare to cross the ocean, either saved for years or signed on ships as redemptioners. A redemptioner signed an agreement with a shipowner or merchant who paid his or her passage. In return, the immigrant worked off the debts in America. Therefore, many came to Vermont not only poor, ragged, and unhealthy but in debt as well.

Irish

The Irish were the first to flow into our state in large numbers. During the nineteenth century, Irish people left their country in larger proportions than any other ethnic group. Their emigration actually caused a decline in the population of their homeland—the only emigration to do so. What could cause so many people to uproot themselves and move across the ocean to a new land?

One big reason was a terrible famine that hit Ireland in 1846. People were suffering terribly, many starving to death. But the Irish had come before the famine and continued to flee their homeland after it. The reasons can be traced back to an English invasion in 1649. The English army had killed or removed thousands of Irish from their land. After pushing the Irish families off their farms, English families moved in. The Irish were forced to rent their farmland from the English. They were not even allowed to speak their own language in public. Discrimination, low wages, few jobs, and civil wars against the English all contributed to Irish emigration.

Many of the Irish who came to Vermont during these early years entered through Canada. As you have already seen, many worked to build the railroads. Others worked as farm hands until they could save enough money to buy farms of their own. (They also worked in industries. See Unit 7.) By 1850, the Irish immigrants in Vermont outnumbered all others.

One thing the Irish brought with them made Vermonters very uncomfortable: their religion. Most of the Irish were Catholics, while most other Vermonters were Protestants. Many people made the Irish feel unwelcome because of this. Some businessmen in Brattleboro would not sell the Irish materials to build a church. In 1874, some Catholic children were not allowed to return to school after attending Mass on a holy day. A Catholic church built in Burlington was destroyed by a fire of suspicious origin in 1838. They met with prejudice and discrimination from one end of the state to the other. It took generations for such discrimination to die out. The Irish were not the only ones to face such treatment, either in their homeland or in Vermont.

French Canadians

The French-speaking people in the Province of Quebec also faced discrimination from English-speaking rulers. Remember from Unit 2 that Quebec (and northern Vermont) had once been ruled by the French. When the English defeated them, only the French government disappeared from Quebec—not the French people. They suffered some of the same treatment as the Irish did. They were given the lowest paying jobs and were not allowed to use their language at work or school. The English generally looked down on them and discriminated against them.

Because of such treatment, some French Canadians came to Vermont during the Revolutionary War to fight for the American cause. Others came to get away from the British soldiers stationed in Canada. Later, rebellion against the British, worn-out soil, and crop failures caused many to move south into Franklin and Orleans counties to farm. Today, descendants of these immigrants have become the major farming group in Vermont. They were the second wave of French speakers to flow into Vermont and become a part of our cultural patchwork. We shall meet the third wave in the next unit.

Other Ethnic Groups

Germans also came to Vermont during the Revolutionary War. The first German immigrants probably were Hessian soldiers, who had been paid by the British to help them during the American Revolution. Some of these German soldiers deserted during the war and came to Highgate, Shelburne, New Haven, and other Champlain Valley towns where they were safe from discovery.

Many more Germans came to America during the nineteenth century to escape misery at home. Crop failures and famines had driven many from their farms. Some of these refugees worked as craftsmen and peddlers until they could save enough money to farm.

Scandinavian farmers also found their way to Vermont. When farmers began to leave the state in droves, the state government decided to do something to save the many abandoned farms in the hills. In the 1890s, Alonzo Valentine, the commissioner of agriculture and manufacturing interests, recruited people from Sweden to live on farms in Wilmington, Weston, and Vershire. Some of the townspeople welcomed the newcomers and provided them with supplies until they were settled. People also were arriving from Finland to farm in the Mount Holly, Ludlow, and Chester area.

Although these immigrants chose to come to America, their move was not without hardship and pain. They were separated from family and friends and had left a familiar lifestyle. They found themselves among unfamiliar customs and a strange language: They no longer "belonged." Some were welcomed into their new communities, but many encountered suspicion and discrimination. Their descendants eventually would feel at home in America and Vermont, but the original immigrants endured much pain and sorrow while pursuing their dreams.

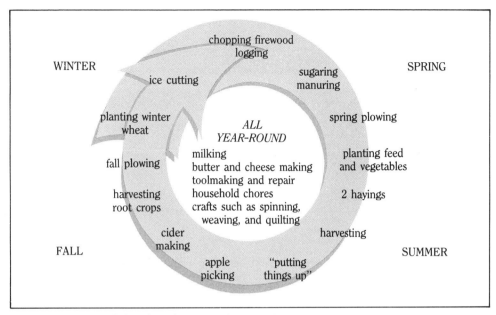

From the heyday of the Abenaki to our dairying days, survival in Vermont has been closely attuned to the changing seasons. This illustration shows the shifting chores according to the dictates of Mother Nature. Farmers of today still perform many of the same chores. The tools may have changed, but nature stays the same. (Adapted from The Vermont Farm Year in 1890, *pp. 2–3)*

Recipe

Irish Soda Bread
(400 °F oven)

4¼ cups flour
2 tablespoons sugar
1 teaspoon salt
1 teaspoon baking soda
½ teaspoon baking powder
¾ cup raisins
2 teaspoons caraway seeds
2 cups buttermilk
1 egg, lightly beaten

1. Mix first 5 ingredients in large bowl.
2. Stir in raisins and caraway seeds.
3. Add buttermilk. Stir with wooden spoon, then hands, to make a sticky dough.
4. Put dough on well-floured surface. Knead about 10 times with floured hands.
5. Shape dough in 3 balls and a stem. Place on greased baking sheet in the form of a shamrock.
6. Brush dough with egg.
7. Cut a ½-inch slash down the center of each "leaf."
8. Bake 35 to 40 minutes, or until golden brown.

Cool and serve with some sweet Vermont butter. It would be even more fun to use butter you have churned yourself!

Story

Coming of Age on a Vermont Farm*

by Richard J. Guyette

Young William Milo Page swung his ax methodically in the late December afternoon chill. He was short and stocky with sandy colored hair, and though Pa had always said he was "too puny to do much farm work," Bill was well muscled at fifteen. As the chunks fell away from the block, they were pushed aside by thirteen-year-old Silas, who centered another piece on the block. Since Pa had last seen the boys, Silas had shot up like a weed and was now taller than Bill. The two worked well and smoothly together, and the chore of splitting went without a break in the rhythm—one moving one way, the other moving the other way in perfect synchrony, like the workings in a clock.

As the sun sank lower toward the western horizon, the pile of split wood seemed to grow to meet it. There was little noise save for the crack of the ax and the consequential clatter of wood on the frozen earth. On this particular December 19, 1864, there was little to be noisy about and much to bury in distracting toil.

For the past three years, the two boys, along with Ma and Silas's twin sister, Delila, had worked their one-hundred-acre farm along the Connecticut River with the help of one orphan boy, Fred Kimball. Pa had joined up with the 6th Vermont Infantry Regiment back in 1861 and had left Fred, who was then sixteen, charged with overseeing the activities of the farm. Pa expected that the Union would put down the rebellion and free the slaves in no more than six months, leaving him to return in time for spring planting. Events didn't quite work out the way he had planned.

Pa wrote as well as he could and as often as he could, but he wasn't much of a hand at writing, and the war didn't always make delivery of mail a priority. In the meantime, the daily routines of farm life moved slowly from day to day, then month to month and year to year. Without Pa, nothing was really the way it should be. Life moved on, but only in anticipation of the day when Pa would come home and make things whole again. After all this time, Bill even began to forget what Pa looked and sounded like. The tintype (photograph) he had sent from Philadelphia didn't help because he looked stiff, uncomfortable, and unfamiliar in his Union uniform and uncharacteristic pose.

Finally, in October 1864, Fred left the farm for Montpelier, where he signed on as a new recruit for the 6th Vermont, which had lost a considerable number of men in the war by that time. The family hadn't heard from Pa since March, and the Rutland *Herald* had carried news of a big battle in Virginia, in May, at a place called The Wilderness, where the 6th had lost 35 killed, 169 wounded, and another 26 who had died later of wounds. It didn't look good for Pa because he tried to write after the big battles to let everyone know he was all right. Anyway, Fred promised he would write as soon as he met up with the 6th and could get some news. Today, two months later, the letter from Fred finally arrived.

Just that afternoon, Charly Haig had ridden out from Thetford Village. He came thundering into the yard just past noon with his horse lathered up enough so that Silas had to take the animal into the barn and rub him down because of the cold. Of course, the entire village knew that Pa hadn't been heard from, so they were all eager for the news, too. Charly wouldn't fail them. He hadn't failed the town in thirty years.

The old clock on the mantle ticked off what seemed to be hours as Ma studied the scratchings on the paper. She was as pale as a sheet when she passed the letter to Bill. Fred's letter was brief. Pa had been shot in the battle of The Wilderness, as was suspected, and someone was to meet the train in White River Junction on December 20. The letter came from Fredericksburg, Virginia, and gave no other clues. If Pa hadn't been killed or maimed, he would have written something to let everyone know he was safe. The news was not good. Christmas 1864 promised to be even bleaker than the last three had been.

There were only traces of orange visible along the top of the stubbled ridge to the west when the boys relented in their assault on the wood. The sky was dark and already sprinkled with the frigid sparkle of winter stars. The warm and fragrant kitchen offered not only food and a welcome respite from the cold but signaled an end to the day's labor. Tonight there was little talk. Ma, still pale, looked haggard and strangely fragile as she served the hearty meal of side pork, white gravy, and johnnycake. Delila was pouring the excess milk of the day into wide, shallow pans from which she would make tomorrow's butter. When she was finished, everyone sat down at the plank table and bowed their heads in prayer.

Bill attempted to get a conversation going by remarking that after he had hauled the month's accumulation of limb wood to the sugar house, he had hitched the oxen to a basswood log he had felled earlier and dragged it down to the barn. He had hoped that he could cheer Ma up with that news because she had wanted a basswood log so she and Delila could bottom the old chairs and make a supply of baskets with the light, durable wood. But Ma just nodded and stared at her work-reddened hands, and Delila and Silas looked too tired to speak. It had been a long day for everyone, even if the winter was, in a way, less work than the other seasons.

Later, while Bill lay on his straw mattress, he reflected on what life would be like without Pa to depend on. True, Pa had been gone three years, but they had always expected him to come home and relieve them of the burden of decision. There were so many things to decide. With roughly eighty good growing days in a year, planting had to be planned carefully. Ashes from the sugarhouse and manure from the barn had to be turned under in the spring as soon as the ground could be worked. The hay crop of herdsgrass and red clover had to be sown early, followed by patches of rye, corn, barley, and wheat for bread. Buckwheat was sown for chicken feed; beans, peas, corn, and ladyfinger potatoes were planted for the cattle and hogs.

Ma and Delila put in the garden crops of popcorn, pole beans, cabbage, cucumbers, onions, squash, rutabagas, pumpkins, carrots, turnips, and pink-eye potatoes. Everything had to be tended and nurtured, priorities had to be set, and the weather had to be on their side. Winter survival for the stock and themselves depended on correct judgment— and luck. While Bill, Silas, and Fred had tended the fields, picked rocks and built walls, cleared land, and cut firewood for the coming year, Ma and Delila had tended the garden crops; tended the cows, pigs, chickens, and sheep; made butter, bread, and soap; dipped candles; wove carpets and quilts; and cared for the house.

In addition to these things, the entire family participated in making maple sugar, butchering, salting and smoking meat, and harvesting apples, nuts, and berries. If they had a surplus, it was sold—maple sugar for 8½ cents per pound and butter for 25 cents per pound. Excess milk was sold to the cheese factory or traded for cheese; excess potatoes were sold to the starch mill; and excess hay and block wood were sold for cash or traded for goods or services. In very good years, beef, pork, and apples also were sold.

None of the day, from sunup until sundown, was wasted. Rainy days were spent on repair and upkeep of the horse-drawn farm equipment, which consisted of a side-hill plow, spring-tooth harrow, weeder, wheel rake, and iron cultivator.

Well, he might just as well start thinking for himself. Pa was gone, and Fred was off to the war. He and Ma had made the decisions for two months and hadn't come up lacking. But she needed him to be stronger now, and he resolved to do just that. He snuggled down deeper under his blankets as the wind wailed around the house like a nervous catamount [wild cat] and was soon deep asleep, unmindful of the rattling and groaning as the old house protested its battering by the winter gale.

The squeaking of the hand pump down in the kitchen woke Bill with a start. Outside, all was silent, and the eastern horizon across the ice-choked Connecticut glowed faintly with the promise of a new day. His feet danced across the cold board floor as he struggled into his clothes. White River Junction was several hours by horse and sleigh. If the snow was deep, he had to take the oxen to break out the road. Bill scraped the frost off the inside of the window and peered outside. It hadn't snowed at all. With the horse, he could make good time.

Ma was in the kitchen with breakfast ready. Bill heard Delila coming down the back stairs and Silas stamping his feet upstairs. He paused in the parlor and picked up the tintype, which was displayed conspicuously on the round oak table. Pa sat stiffly on a stool gazing straight ahead, his expression faintly amused. His tunic was buttoned to the neck, left leg crossed over the right at the ankle, right forearm resting casually on a small covered table next to his cap.

In a way, the picture captured something Bill had never fully realized. Pa was proud to be a soldier for the Union, but at the same time, his expression said, "Why are we wasting time with this? Let's get on with the fight." Bill suddenly remembered that about Pa—good-natured with a sense of humor but determined to get to the task at hand. If Bill was going to help Ma run the farm successfully, he was going to have to possess the same qualities, and deep down inside he knew that. Vermont boys and girls learned young about dealing with the unexpected. Nature could turn on you at any time with floods, high winds, or deep snows. Injuries and illness or sudden death were part of life, and you had to stand up under the burden and then fling it from you and go on.

Bill carefully put the tintype on the table and turned toward the kitchen, where only the murmur of voices and the sputtering of the coal oil lamps could be heard. Outside the parlor window, last year's leaves began to rattle in the red oak tree as the wind quickened before the dawn. The day was about to begin in uncertainty, and they all must accept what the day brought them as they had accepted what other days had brought. It could be no other way. It was the price one paid for life. Whether the day brought sorrow or happiness, they would go on and face each new day with increased confidence. That's what Pa would want. They wouldn't disappoint him.

*Reprinted by permission of Richard J. Guyette.

UNIT 7

The Rhythms of Machines

In the span of one century, Vermont had changed in appearance once again. No longer could change be measured in the often-unnoticed movements of the sluggish earth. Farmers had arrived, and change sped over Vermont's hills and through its villages like wildfire. Steamboats and trains chugged into the state. The once-green hills were being stripped of their trees; otters were disappearing from Otter Creek; the slow-witted turkeys and lightning-quick falcons were leaving; the salmon, shad, and moose were vanishing.

During the nineteenth century, industry contributed to the changes started by the new forms of transportation and farming. Slowly but surely, Vermont green became dappled with gray from factory smokestacks. For many, it was a sign of prosperity, a sign that people were working. Even though much of the land was worn-out, families could still make a living in the cities. The quiet rhythms of nature and the seasons began to give way to the rhythms of machines.

The abandonment of the hill farms caused a nineteen percent decrease in the population of Vermont's rural areas. Yet the overall population of the state increased by more than twelve percent. How did this happen? Thousands of people were pouring into the cities and large towns where industries needed laborers. Some were Yankees who moved into town from the farms; most were immigrants from Canada or faraway countries across the sea. The sounds of the factory whistles calling them to work were the sounds of a new way of life dawning in our state.

Historical Background

From one end of the state to the other, Vermont is marked by rivers, lakes, and streams. Waterpower ran mills and machines and gave life to many small towns. Transportation on the waterways brought new people to replace those migrating to the West. Water vessels carried Vermont-made products to the markets in faraway cities and returned with goods not grown or manufactured here. Later in the century, railroad transportation replaced steamboats, but harnessed waterpower continued to run the industries.

Wood

The largest body of water in Vermont is Lake Champlain. It is not surprising that it became the center of trade at the beginning of the nineteenth century. If industrialists could get their products to the lake, they could join in the bustling trade with Canada. Vermont's most important natural resource to be traded in the early part of the century was trees.

Vermont still had great untouched tracks of forests, especially in the north. French Canadian immigrants formed a large part of Vermont's lumberjack force. The silence of the winter was shattered by the sounds of axes and crashing trees. The lumbermen

BIRD'S EYEVIEW
NEWPORT, VT.
1881.

Bird's-eye views were done by traveling artists. It took a special talent to draw a view as if seen from an airplane—when the airplane had not yet been invented. Notice how bare the surrounding hills are. What caused this? (Special Collections University of Vermont Library)

made huge rafts from the logs in preparation for spring. At that time, the ice went out of the rivers and millions of square feet of spruce and fir were driven downstream to sawmills. The lumber left the state by way of Lake Champlain or the Connecticut River.

Thousands of logs were driven to collection points. Burlington became a major collection and distribution point on Lake Champlain for lumber and other goods. Lumber was bought by shipbuilders along the lake or moved to Canada along the Richelieu River.

Trade with our Canadian neighbors slowed before and during the War of 1812. The war was fought, in part, to protest British stopping of American ships and kidnapping of American sailors they claimed were British. Due to the importance of Vermont's trade with Canada, many Vermonters refused to take part in the war, and some towns refused to raise money for the militia. Governor Martin Chittenden ordered Vermont soldiers back from the western side of Lake Champlain, saying that they should defend only Vermont's borders. The soldiers stayed, however, and took part in the Battle of Plattsburgh, which turned back a British invasion.

Although trade with Canada had been forbidden, Vermonters carried on a healthy smuggling operation across the border. Smugglers' Notch in Lamoille County was named for such activity through a dangerous section of the Green Mountains. After the war, trade again picked up on the lake.

By 1840, the lumber trade had helped make Burlington the largest town in Vermont. But soon Vermont's lumber resource almost disappeared. Only one-quarter of Vermont's forests remained by the mid-1800s, and the timber trade reversed directions, as Vermont started importing Canadian timber. Burlington turned to collecting and finishing the wood. By 1873, Burlington was third in the nation in the production of finished lumber.

By the end of the century, the ever-present competition from the West and planing mills in Canada helped to halt this booming business. But other businesses had grown up in the "Queen City." Industry in Burlington included more than half of Ver-

At the Vermont Marble Company (about 1880), oxen haul marble to the shop where it will be shaped by carvers. (Courtesy the Vermont Marble Company, Proctor, Vermont)

mont's glass producers and one-third of its potteries. They helped Burlington recover from the death of the lumber business, and it has remained Vermont's largest city to this day.

Stone

Other cities and towns grew up around industries based on mineral resources laid down millions of years ago. The first marble quarry in the United States was opened near Dorset in 1785 by Isaac Underhill. The industry stayed small and unimpressive until the next century, when the railroads connected Vermont to faraway markets. Quarries began to open and operate in Sutherland Falls (now Proctor), West Rutland, Rochester, Danby, and other locations with the help of thousands of immigrants. By 1870, Redfield Proctor had brought many of these small companies together to form the Sutherland Falls Marble Company. In the 1880s, the company was renamed the Vermont Marble Company and became the largest corporation in the state.

In the early days, gunpowder and saws were used to loosen the marble from its bed. Log rollers pulled by oxen moved the chunks to the shop to be shaped by hand. Today, diesel-powered lifts are used to haul the marble, and computers are used to shape, cut, and polish it.

People from all over the world have made the Vermont Marble Company the largest marble production center in North America. The Imperial Mine in Danby is the world's largest underground mine. Vermont marble is used from the Supreme Court building in Washington, D.C., to the Chiang Kai-Shek Memorial in Taiwan (Asia).

Another world-famous industry was built from the granite in Washington County. The first quarry was opened in Barre in 1813. The industry grew very slowly until the railroad linked Vermont with larger markets outside the state. In 1880, Barre's population was between two thousand and three thousand. That year, the first experienced Scottish stonecutters arrived, followed in the next few decades by thousands more immigrants.

They built the granite industry and other industries that moved to the swiftly growing town. By 1910, the population of Barre City had mushroomed to more than ten thousand.

By the turn of the century, Barre had more than fifty granite firms and many "sheds," where the fine-grained granite was carved into monuments to be sent all over the world. One quarry was owned by George Milne from Aberdeen, Scotland. He later joined with two Yankees to form the Boutwell, Milne and Varnum Company, which became Rock of Ages. Rock of Ages today boasts the world's largest granite quarry. It is three hundred fifty feet deep and covers twenty acres.

Vermont also became a leading producer of slate, needed as fireproof roofing. In 1839, Alonson Allen opened a mine in Fair Haven. He specialized in making school slates and later turned to roof slates. Like the other stone industries, this one grew slowly until the latter part of the nineteenth century. At that time, master slateworkers from Wales were invited to come and work in Vermont's "slate belt": Fair Haven, Castleton, and Poultney. The Welsh, along with the Irish, were largely responsible for the growth of the slate industry in Vermont.

By the beginning of the twentieth century, Vermont was first in the nation in the production of marble, granite, and asbestos. It was the country's second largest producer of slate, soapstone, and talc. But these were not the only resources plentiful in Vermont. Vermonters themselves also were a great resource. Their ingenuity created great industries, some known worldwide.

Textiles, Tools, and Scales

During the heyday of merino sheep in Vermont, the textile industry sprouted. Small mills and factories sprang up all over the state. A mill took the raw wool (or cotton) and prepared spun yarn. A factory wove the yarn into cloth and may have made the cloth into finished products. Before the end of "merino mania," smaller companies were coming together to form larger ones. When the mania ended, the textile firms were forced to import wool from outside the state. Soon the industry was in trouble.

Something happened, however, that would turn the industry around. The most devastating war our country has ever experienced occurred: the Civil War (see Unit 8). Suddenly, the demand for wool blankets and uniforms shot up, and sixty-nine Vermont firms worked full tilt during the war.

After the war, many of the smaller firms went out of business, but the larger, more efficient ones continued to prosper. The town of Bennington had the most factories (twelve). The largest mills were in Hartford, Ludlow, Cavendish, and Winooski (part of Colchester at that time). Powered by the ancient Winooski River, the Winooski Woolen Mills turned that city into the textile center of the state. A Burlington factory did the weaving. The gigantic Winooski Mill used over 1.2 million pounds of wool a year.

By the end of the century, about six thousand men, women, and children (many of them immigrants) worked in the Vermont textile industry. The mills and factories continued to prosper well into the twentieth century, when it became cheaper to manufacture in the southern United States. Today, you can find old mills in many Vermont towns. Some stand empty—silent monuments to a once-thriving industry. Others have been remade into apartment houses or shopping centers.

The development of the U.S. machine tool and scale industries was dominated by Vermonters in the nineteenth century. One reason for this was that Vermonters con-

Major 19th-Century Vermont Industries

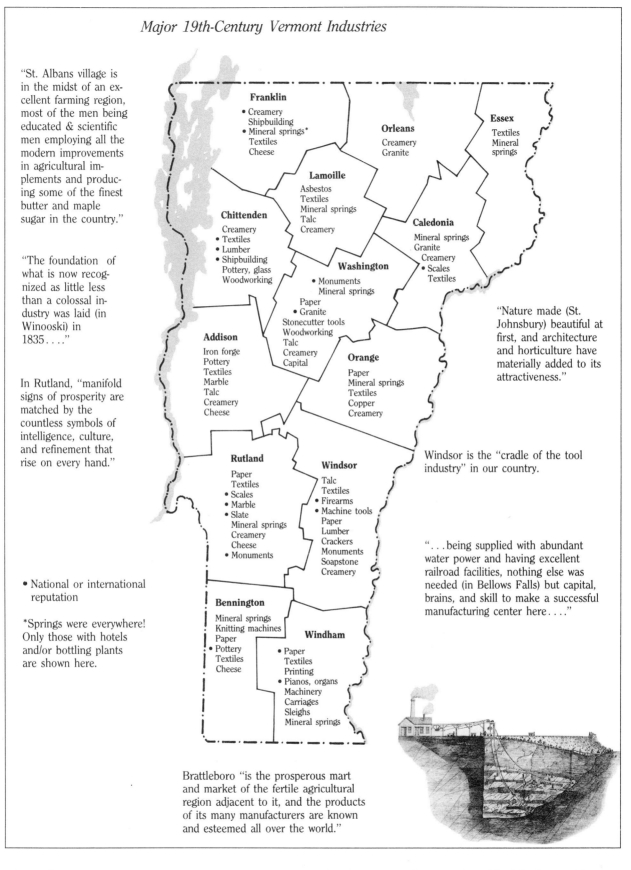

"St. Albans village is in the midst of an excellent farming region, most of the men being educated & scientific men employing all the modern improvements in agricultural implements and producing some of the finest butter and maple sugar in the country."

"The foundation of what is now recognized as little less than a colossal industry was laid (in Winooski) in 1835...."

In Rutland, "manifold signs of prosperity are matched by the countless symbols of intelligence, culture, and refinement that rise on every hand."

• National or international reputation

*Springs were everywhere! Only those with hotels and/or bottling plants are shown here.

Franklin
• Creamery
Shipbuilding
• Mineral springs*
Textiles
Cheese

Orleans
Creamery
Granite

Essex
Textiles
Mineral springs

Lamoille
Asbestos
Textiles
Mineral springs
Talc
Creamery

Chittenden
Creamery
• Textiles
• Lumber
• Shipbuilding
Pottery, glass
Woodworking

Caledonia
Mineral springs
Granite
Creamery
• Scales
Textiles

Washington
• Monuments
Mineral springs
Paper
• Granite
Stonecutter tools
Woodworking
Talc
Creamery
Capital

Addison
Iron forge
Pottery
Textiles
Marble
Talc
Creamery
Cheese

Orange
Paper
Mineral springs
Textiles
Copper
Creamery

"Nature made (St. Johnsbury) beautiful at first, and architecture and horticulture have materially added to its attractiveness."

Rutland
Paper
Textiles
• Scales
• Marble
• Slate
Mineral springs
Creamery
Cheese
• Monuments

Windsor
Talc
Textiles
• Firearms
• Machine tools
Paper
Lumber
Crackers
Monuments
Soapstone
Creamery

Windsor is the "cradle of the tool industry" in our country.

"...being supplied with abundant water power and having excellent railroad facilities, nothing else was needed (in Bellows Falls) but capital, brains, and skill to make a successful manufacturing center here...."

Bennington
Mineral springs
Knitting machines
Paper
• Pottery
Textiles
Cheese

Windham
• Paper
Textiles
Printing
• Pianos, organs
Machinery
Carriages
Sleighs
Mineral springs

Brattleboro "is the prosperous mart and market of the fertile agricultural region adjacent to it, and the products of its many manufacturers are known and esteemed all over the world."

(Quotes from the American Publishing and Engraving Co., New York, 1891 report: Industries and Wealth of the Principal Points in Vermont, Being Burlington, Winooski, Rutland, etc.)

Inset This poster, done about 1857, shows a cross section of a slate quarry. (Photo Special Collections University of Vermont Library)

Note

The original rotating pump was invented by John Cooper of Guildhall. Notice how inventions evolve as one inventor builds on the ideas of another.

Note

Name changes of the major machine tool company: National Hydraulic (1828); Robbins, Lawrence & Kendall (1846); Lamson & Goodnow (1858); Windsor Manufacturing Company (after the war); Jones & Lamson (1876 to present).

Note

Hemp is a plant with tough fibers used to make rope.

tributed many of the important inventions. The machine tool industry was born in Windsor in 1828. The National Hydraulic Company was formed to make Asahel Hubbard's revolving hydraulic engine (an improved water pump with interchangeable parts). The laborers who laid the foundation for this amazing industry were the convicts at the Windsor Prison, where Hubbard was the warden. In 1835, his son-in-law, Nicanor Kendall, invented an improved rifle-firing hammer, and the convicts proceeded to produce the Kendall rifle.

In the 1840s, the company moved out of the prison. The firm continued to grow, changing its name several times. It produced sewing machines, punch presses, and various tools. With increasing hostilities during the Civil War, the industry thrived by producing more than one hundred fifty thousand small arms, including fifty thousand .58-caliber muskets.

After the war, the company fell on hard times and was sold to a group of Springfield businessmen. They hired James Hartness to run the company and moved it to the banks of the Black River in Springfield in 1888. In the years after the move, Hartness invented and perfected the turret lathe—a machine used for shaping wood or metal with a rotating block (turret) holding several cutting tools. His invention revolutionized the machine tool industry. Until 1904, Springfield, Vermont, was the only place in the world where you could purchase a turret lathe.

Springfield became a major manufacturing center in the twentieth century, employing thousands of people, many of them immigrants. Their product was important to the nation, especially during World Wars I and II. Through this industry, begun in the state prison in 1828, Vermonters gained a fine reputation as makers of quality machines.

While the machine tool industry was being built in southern Vermont, another Vermont industry was taking hold on the Sleepers River in St. Johnsbury. In 1821, Thaddeus Fairbanks patented his invention of the platform scale. He invented it so farmers could weigh hemp more accurately but discovered it could weigh just about anything, including railroad cars. Along with his brother, Erastus, he formed the E&T Fairbanks Company to manufacture the scales. It was the first such company in the United States. By the 1840s, the scales were being sold from Cuba to China.

In 1865, one hundred miles southwest of St. Johnsbury, Frank Strongs invented another scale. The Vergennes man's scale was mounted on ball bearings (instead of levers like the Fairbanks scale). The Howe Scale Company of Brandon manufactured this new scale until the building burned down in 1873. Four years later, John Howe opened his new scale company in Rutland. It became a major industry in that county.

The reputation of Vermont scales spread throughout the country and continued into the twentieth century. As late as the 1950s, Vermonters in St. Johnsbury and Rutland were producing three-quarters of all the scales in the nation. It did not make business sense that these large items were produced so far away from city markets. Usually parts of larger items are made in out-of-the-way places, shipped to city markets, and put together there. Vermont's machine tool and scale companies worked in the opposite direction because of the inventiveness of Vermonters. But they could not keep working against the flow forever. Today, the Howe Scale works in Rutland stands empty, and the old Fairbanks Scale Company is gone. In its place stands a modern division of Colt Industries, which makes industrial weighing equipment.

The People Who Built Our Industrial Tradition

During the first half of the nineteenth century, mostly native-born Vermonters worked in the fledgling industries. By mid-century, however, many new immigrants were braving the dangers of an ocean crossing to find new opportunities in the United States. Most of these immigrants came in poverty and poor health, and they were uneducated and unskilled. For many, Vermont held the answers to their hopes and dreams for the future.

Irish

In Unit 6, we explored why the Irish left their homeland in such great numbers. They believed that America was a place where they could escape starvation and persecution. So many came to Vermont that by 1850, they had become the largest immigrant group in the state, numbering fifteen thousand.

Note

A monopoly is the exclusive control of a business.

The Irish were said to form a "monopoly of the pick and shovel." They built our roads, dug our canals, and laid our eastern railroad lines. (In the West, Chinese workers built the railroad.) As more and more came, they found work in the mills, quarries, and factories. The Irish were the first immigrant quarrymen in the Vermont marble industry.

Aside from the religious discrimination discussed in Unit 6, the Irish encountered discrimination in the workplace. Since they were so poor when they came to this country, the company owners figured they would work for less money than the Yankees. The owners were right; the immigrants accepted whatever was offered to them. Gradually, many Yankees were pushed out of the work force or had to accept lower wages. As you can imagine, this caused bitter feelings toward the Irish. It took many years for the Yankees and Irish to join together to fight for higher wages.

French Canadians

The next flow of immigrants to wash over Vermont came from the north. The French were the first whites to settle in Vermont, and French Canadians have never stopped immigrating here. During the nineteenth century, however, the numbers were especially high. What caused so much unrest among French Canadians?

After Canada became part of the British Empire (1763), the French-speaking people gradually became a minority in the Province of Quebec. They were discriminated against in many ways by the English. To escape prejudice and find employment, many French Canadians came to work in Vermont industries. After the Civil War, sixty thousand to seventy-five thousand came to Chittenden County alone to work in the mills and factories. They were said to have *le mal des Etats-Unis* (sickness for the United States).

Note

A strike is a refusal to work until an agreement is made between workers and owners.

Can you guess what happened when the French Canadians came to the factories to work? It happened with the Irish and would happen again with each group of immigrants. The owners again offered the newcomers lower wages, which they had to accept to get a job. If the old immigrants (Irish and Yankees) went on strike for higher wages, many owners went to Quebec to recruit workers. The owners paid the immigrants' train fares and brought them into Vermont full of hope for a new life. Of course, what awaited them was anger and discrimination, and bitter friction between the French Canadians and the Irish and Yankee workers lasted for some time.

Like all immigrant groups, the French Canadians tended to stay together in their neighborhoods where there was a sense of belonging. They could speak their own language and practice their customs without interference. The first French-language newspaper in New England was established in Burlington in 1839.

When the French Canadians wanted to form their own Catholic parishes, the Irish objected. By this time, the Irish were very powerful in the Church and did not want to give up their power to these newcomers. After a fight with the Irish Catholics that went all the way to the pope in Rome, the first French parish in New England was established in Burlington in 1850.

Despite their difficulties at first, French Canadian immigrants held on to their culture and prospered. Today, they are the largest minority group in Vermont, adding a great deal to the diversity of the cultural landscape.

Italians

In 1850, there were seven Italians in Vermont. By 1910, there were more than forty-five hundred—the fourth largest immigrant group in the state. Italians (mostly from southern Italy) left their homeland for familiar reasons. In Italy, they had rented their land at very high prices. The soil was worn-out, and the farmers lived in poverty. Discontent with their government and overpopulation also contributed to large Italian emigrations. Most of them came to America in poverty with no education or industrial skills. Their fares were paid by a *padrone*, or labor boss, in return for a part of their wages in America.

One of the first groups of Italians to come to Vermont, however, did not come in poverty, nor were they unskilled. In 1882, Redfield Proctor of the Vermont Marble Company invited a group of master marble carvers from northern Italy to work for him. They worked as carvers and taught their skills to other marbleworkers.

Many carvers, quarrymen, and businessmen followed this first group to the Rutland-Proctor area, and even more Italians went to Barre to work in the granite industry. By 1910, half the population of "The Granite Capital of the World" was Italian. They gave Vermonters their first taste of southern European culture. Many Spanish people escaping civil war in Spain also brought a Mediterranean influence to the state.

Welsh

Another group of master craftsmen came to the Poultney area in the late 1800s to work in the slate industry. In Wales, the English refused to let the Welsh use their own language or own land or homes. They worked long hours in the mines under terrible conditions. As a result, many were quite happy to come to Vermont when invited. They did not come in the thousands like the other ethnic groups but were considered the aristocrats (nobles) of the labor force.

Eastern Europeans (Slavs)

At the turn of the century, more people with new customs and languages found their way to Vermont. This time Polish, Russian, and Hungarian echoed in the Green Mountains. By 1920, more than thirty-four hundred Slavic people lived in the state.

They had left their homeland for the same reasons as most other immigrants: poverty, unemployment, worn-out soil, and discrimination. The largest group, the Poles, were governed by the Russian tsar (king or emperor), who would not allow them to practice many of their customs. Both the Poles and Russians were forced into military service and wished to escape this ordeal.

Many of them were Jewish people who were persecuted for their religion. In Europe, Christian Slavs often would attack Jewish *shetetls* (villages), massacring the inhabitants and destroying their homes. These attacks were called pogroms and were encouraged by the government. An underground railroad (much like the one in the United States that helped escaped slaves prior to the Civil War) helped Jewish people make their way to other parts of Europe and the United States. German Jews had established the first Jewish settlement in Vermont near Poultney in the mid-1800s. The largest Jewish community, however, was founded by Russian Jews in Burlington.

Many Jews became traveling peddlers. They bought local goods such as cloth, kitchen utensils, and tinware. They then filled their wagons with the goods and sold them to customers at their homes. Some became tinkers, who traveled around fixing things in people's homes. Poultney became a meeting place for these peddlers and tinkers.

Both the Polish and Russian immigrants were attracted to the machine tool industry in Springfield. Many Poles also moved to West Rutland to work in the marble industry.

In addition to the Slavs, many Christians from Greece and Lebanon immigrated to northern Vermont. They, too, were escaping religious persecution under the Muslim Turkish Empire.

Note

"Homogeneous" means everywhere the same.

As you can see, immigrants brought a great deal of their cultures with them when they came to Vermont. Their new languages and customs brought diversity to a once-homogeneous state. By 1900, the majority of Vermont's industrial workers were foreign born. It is hard to imagine what would have happened in Vermont if they had not come.

Working Conditions

We cannot leave this section without exploring the conditions in the workplace. Concern about these conditions was voiced in Vermont in many different languages, and it is something that still concerns Vermonters today.

Each group of workers came to Vermont with the hope of improving its members' lot in life. When they arrived, they found jobs at very low pay. They worked long hours—twelve to thirteen hours a day, six days a week—for as little as one dollar a day, and everyone in the family had to work to pay the bills.

In the textile mills, workers had to be at their machines when the machines started and could not leave them until they stopped hours later. Starting and stopping of the machines was controlled by the bosses. Sometimes the air became so thick with wool or cotton dust it was hard to breathe. These fibers caused byssinosis, or

Addie Laird was 10 years old when she worked full-time in a Pownal textile mill. (Courtesy of the Library of Congress)

Copper miners (c. 1880) work underground by the dim light of kerosene lamps. Many of the miners were immigrants from Cornwall, England. (Special Collections University of Vermont Library)

brown lung disease. The windows stayed closed, even on the hottest summer days, because threads broke less often in humid air.

People in the quarrying industries worked under the same type of conditions. They had the same long hours and low pay, and they risked their lives everyday. Quarrying was dangerous work, and occasionally men died in dynamite explosions or were crushed under huge chunks of marble or granite. Marble dust in the carving sheds caused tuberculosis; granite dust caused silicosis. Both are diseases of the lungs that killed many quarrymen at a young age.

The immigrants still dreamed of jobs where working conditions were healthy and the pay was high enough to save for a home and some land. As the workers labored for low wages, they watched the factory owners and their families getting richer. Soon they started demanding more. The words "union" and "collective bargaining" were heard for the first time. Workers talked about uniting to ask for better pay and working conditions. As early as the 1830s, *The Working Man's Gazette* was published complaining of the inequality between workers and owners, and workers' societies were calling for better wages.

Note
The first strike in America was by Polish craftsmen in Jamestown, Virginia, in 1619. It was successful.

Sometimes they had to unite to get paid at all. A group of Irish railroad workers in Richmond staged the first strike in Vermont in 1846. They had not been paid in two months and took one of the contractors hostage. His partner went for the money but returned with the Burlington Light Infantry. The leaders of the strike were dragged off to jail, and many workers never received their pay.

In 1855, Brattleboro washerwomen went on strike until they were promised seventy-five cents for twelve pieces of laundry. Women textile workers in Woodstock went on strike for a ten-hour day in 1866. Cornish and Irish copper miners in Ely (Vershire)

Note

"To smelt" means to melt metal.

had not been paid for months when they went on strike in June 1883. When the owners refused to pay them unless they smelted the ore already mined, the strikers threatened to burn the village. The state militia was called in to subdue the men. Eventually, they collected only about twenty percent of their back wages. Most moved away to find other jobs, and soon after, the company closed down for good.

In Barre and Proctor, miners voted in the late nineteenth century to have national unions represent them when talking to the owners. By 1900, about twenty percent of the marbleworkers were unionized. A short strike in Proctor in 1904 was not successful but did improve relations for a while, as the owners voluntarily decided to improve working conditions. They started company stores, a women's center, and a free hospital. At the same time, ninety percent of the Barre workers were unionized. There were no strikes in Barre until 1922. Despite the small gains made by workers, by 1910, wages in Vermont ranked thirty-sixth out of forty-six states. Vermonters became increasingly dissatisfied with their standing, and they took more action on the labor front in the twentieth century (Section III).

Activity

A Paper-Cutting Activity
(18)

The Polish word for paper cutting is *wycinanki* (vi·chee·nán·kee). The Poles (and many others in eastern Europe and Asia) enjoy making paper cutouts to decorate their homes. In earlier times, the Poles painted the designs or used leather for the cutouts.

Try your hand at some of these colorful pieces of art. All you need are colored paper (construction, wrapping, or origami), a pencil, scissors, and some glue.

1. Fold a piece of paper in half.
2. Either trace or design your own pattern on half the paper.
3. Cut out the pattern. Unfold. You now have your first layer.

1   2   layer one
                                                                                                              3

4. Make some more layers, each smaller than the next, to paste on the original layer.

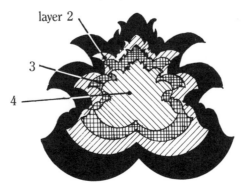

layer 2

3

4

5. You can make animals or more elaborate designs for wall hangings or bookmarks. Don't be afraid to experiment!

Recipe

Pizza—Italian

Crust:

1 package active dry yeast
¾ cup warm water
2½ cups biscuit mix
olive oil (or other salad oil)
Pizza sauce (can or jar)

Favorite Pizza Toppings:

Mozzarella cheese
Pepperoni
Mushrooms
Onions
Peppers
Anchovies
Italian sausage (cooked)

1. Soften yeast in warm water.
2. Add biscuit mix. Beat vigorously for 2 minutes.
3. Knead dough until smooth. Add more biscuit mix if needed.
4. Divide dough in half. Roll into two 12-inch circles.
5. Place dough on greased baking sheets; crimp edges. Brush with oil.
6. Cover with pizza sauce and other pizza toppings. Bake 15 minutes in a 425°F oven.

Recipe

Sugar Pie
(a traditional French Canadian recipe*)

unbaked pie crust
¼ to ½ cup butter
1 cup dark brown sugar
   or maple syrup
¼ cup flour

2 cups milk or 1 cup milk and 1 cup sour cream
1 teaspoon vanilla
pinch of cinnamon and nutmeg

1. Mix sugar and flour. Pour into pie crust.
2. Mix milk and vanilla. Pour over sugar mixture. Dot with butter.
3. Sprinkle with spices.
4. Bake: Pyrex dish—375°F for 10 minutes
                325°F for 35 minutes
     Tin dish—350°F for 40 to 45 minutes

*Donated by Liette Charron of St. Albans, Vermont

UNIT 8

Vermonters Influence Their Nation

Let's stop for a moment and think back over the ups and downs of the nineteenth century. Thousands of people had moved to Vermont after statehood to farm. They built homes and raised families. When the soil began to wear out, thousands of Vermonters abandoned the state for the western prairies. People lost friends and family members in these great migrations. Then once again, thousands of newcomers came to Vermont seeking a new way of life. They brought new languages and customs from far away. It was a difficult and painful journey away from their homelands, families, and friends. They were happy just to find work, but the hours were long and the conditions poor. Life was not easy for people in those days.

Even with all these difficulties, Vermonters found time to think of others who needed a helping hand. Many men and women risked their own freedom by working secretly on the Underground Railroad, which helped runaway slaves from the South to freedom in Canada. Thousands of Vermonters fought in the Civil War, partly because of the slavery issue. Other people stepped forward to work for women's rights and children's education rights. A powerful voice pleading for preservation of our environment was first heard in Vermont. In this unit, we will meet some of the spirited men and women who raised their voices to convert many of their compatriots to these worthy causes.

None of these new ideas was introduced into our state or our country without problems. As you probably have noticed by now, change cannot be stopped, but people do not always like it. All the issues in this unit are still being debated today in different forms. Let's look at what form they took in the nineteenth century.

Abolition of Slavery

All the immigrant groups mentioned so far came to America voluntarily, looking for freedom. Thousands of immigrants, however, were forced to come and lost their freedom in the process. The first group of black people to arrive in America came to Jamestown, Virginia, in 1619. They probably came as servants, not slaves. The institution of slavery grew slowly as the plantations in the South grew. The subsequent history of slavery in America is long and filled with misery.

Although Vermont was not a slave state, its inhabitants had a great interest in the issue. As you may remember, Vermont was the first state to outlaw slavery. When the Green Mountain Boys took Fort Ticonderoga during the American Revolution, they found a British slave and her child. Everyone agreed to set them free, and Ebenezer Allen wrote a certificate of freedom for them. In another case in the early 1800s, an escaped slave had made his way to Middlebury to live as a free man. His "owner" had followed him and demanded that his "property" be returned. The case went to court. Judge Theophilus Harrington told the southerner that if he produced a "bill of sale

Note

Many black patriots fought in the American Revolution, and some joined the Green Mountain Boys in Vermont.

from Almighty God," the black man would be returned to him. Needless to say, the southerner went away empty-handed.

Judge Harrington was disobeying a 1793 U.S. law that gave slave holders the right to recapture escaped slaves. In 1843, Vermont passed a law making it illegal to recapture escapees. Vermonters again were defying the laws of the land. Civil disobedience was alive and well in the Green Mountains.

Those who chose to work within the law had other methods. By the 1830s, Vermont had many antislavery groups and four antislavery newspapers. The town of Bennington sent more than twenty-three hundred signatures to Washington, D.C., demanding the abolition of slavery there. The first abolitionist speech heard in Congress was given by Vermonter William Slade.

Despite such actions, the U.S. Congress passed the Fugitive Slave Act in 1850, which punished people who aided slaves with imprisonment and fines. Vermonters responded by declaring any slave brought into the state to be a free person. They backed up their words with actions by participating in the intricate Underground Railroad. This was not a real railroad with tracks and trains. It was made up of secret paths traveled at night and houses with secret rooms to hide runaway slaves. Every person along the route was disobeying the laws of the United States.

The men and women who risked imprisonment believed that the rights of human beings were more important than their own safety. Imagine Vermonters, tired after a long day of working, setting out from their homes under cover of night. Perhaps they would be in a hay wagon pretending to visit a neighbor. But the wagon actually was for hiding a runaway—someone scared to death of the slave hunters who followed. The white "conductor" on the Underground Railroad transported the frightened runaway to yet another secret room behind a secret panel, or perhaps the former slave slept on the floor in a cellar or barn. While the runaway was in hiding, Vermont families took care of his or her needs. They provided food, clothing, and medical attention until it was time for the runaway to move on to the next station.

One house along the way was Rokeby—the home of Rachael and Rowland T. Robinson of Ferrisburg. They had built a secret room above their kitchen. Many slaves on Vermont's western route spent a night in that room on their way to freedom in Canada. The house is now a museum, where you can stand in the same room where many courageous human beings hid from their captors.

All of this activity in Vermont caused the Georgia state senate to ask President Franklin Pierce (1853–1857) to "employ a sufficient number of able-bodied Irishmen to proceed to the State of Vermont, and to dig a ditch around the limits of the same, and to float 'the thing' into the Atlantic."* Vermonters paid no attention to such mudslinging. In 1860, they went to the polls to vote for the sixteenth president of the United States. Abraham Lincoln was the antislavery candidate. Stephen Douglas, a Vermonter for the first twenty years of his life, was in favor of compromise. He thought each state should resolve the slavery issue for itself. Two other candidates were proslavery. When the ballots were counted, Vermonters had given Lincoln 75.8 percent of their votes. Douglas received 19.4 percent and the proslavery candidates 4.68 percent. They had voted against a native son for a noble cause.

*William Doyle, *The Vermont Political Tradition* (Barre, Vermont: Northlight Studio Press, 1984), p. 114.

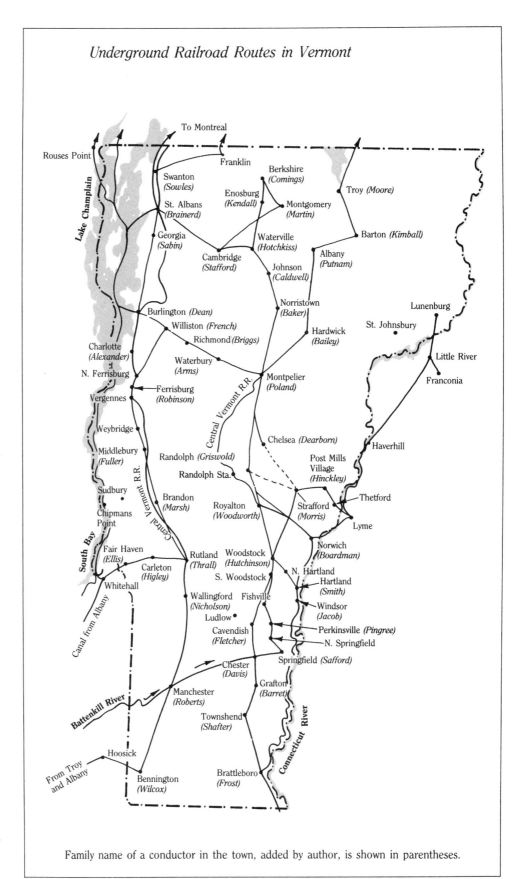

Underground Railroad Routes in Vermont

To Montreal

Rouses Point

Lake Champlain

Franklin

Swanton
(Sowles)

Berkshire
(Comings)

Enosburg
(Kendall)

Troy *(Moore)*

St. Albans
(Brainerd)

Montgomery
(Martin)

Georgia
(Sabin)

Waterville
(Hotchkiss)

Barton *(Kimball)*

Cambridge
(Stafford)

Albany
(Putnam)

Johnson
(Caldwell)

Lunenburg

Norristown
(Baker)

Burlington *(Dean)*

St. Johnsbury

Williston *(French)*

Richmond *(Briggs)*

Hardwick
(Bailey)

Little River

Charlotte
(Alexander)

Waterbury
(Arms)

Franconia

N. Ferrisburg

Montpelier
(Poland)

Ferrisburg
(Robinson)

Vergennes

Central Vermont R.R.

Weybridge

Chelsea *(Dearborn)*

Haverhill

Middlebury
(Fuller)

Randolph *(Griswold)*

Post Mills
Village
(Hinckley)

Randolph Sta.

Thetford

Sudbury

Brandon
(Marsh)

Strafford
(Morris)

Chipmans
Point

Royalton
(Woodworth)

Lyme

Central Vermont R.R.

South Bay

Fair Haven
(Ellis)

Rutland
(Thrall)

Woodstock
(Hutchinson)

Norwich
(Boardman)

Carleton
(Higley)

S. Woodstock

N. Hartland

Whitehall

Hartland
(Smith)

Wallingford
(Nicholson)

Fishville

Ludlow

Windsor
(Jacob)

Canal from Albany

Cavendish
(Fletcher)

Perkinsville *(Pingree)*

N. Springfield

Springfield *(Safford)*

Chester
(Davis)

Grafton
(Barret)

Manchester
(Roberts)

Battenkill River

Townshend
(Shafter)

Connecticut River

Hoosick

From Troy
and Albany

Bennington
(Wilcox)

Brattleboro
(Frost)

Family name of a conductor in the town, added by author, is shown in parentheses.

*Wilbur H. Siebert,
Vermont's Anti-Slavery
and Underground Rail-
road Record (Columbus,
Ohio: The Spahr and
Glenn Company, 1937.)*

The spread between the votes cast for Lincoln and Douglas was not as large in other states. Douglas lost the election by fewer than half a million votes. Obviously, there was a great split in the nation over this issue.

Within a year after the election, the southern states had left the Union and formed the Confederate States of America. The opening shots of the Civil War were fired on April 12, 1861, at Fort Sumter in Charleston, South Carolina.

Civil War

Note

The Emancipation Procla- mation, effective January 1, 1863, freed all slaves in the states still at war with the Union.

Note

The Confederates' famous charge is known as Pickett's charge in honor of General George Pickett.

More than twenty-four thousand Vermonters rallied to the call to fight to save the Union. The Vermont Brigade was considered one of the best in the entire Union army. It was the only one in the Union army named after a state, quite an honor. The brigade participated in all the major battles in Virginia, Maryland, and Pennsylvania. Two of its more important battles were at Gettysburg, Pennsylvania, and The Wilderness in Virginia.

In 1862, the Vermont Brigade fought in the bloodiest day of fighting in the war: the battle of Antietam in Maryland, which led to Lincoln's Emancipation Proclamation. With the experience gained there and in other clashes, the Vermonters saved the day at Gettysburg the following year.

After two days of horrifying fighting at Gettysburg, it appeared that the Confederates, under General Robert E. Lee, were finally overrunning the Union line. George G. Meade, the Union general, sent in his best troops—the Vermont Brigade—to halt the attack. Led by General George Stannard of St. Albans, they broke the rebel charge and turned the tide of the battle. One of the South's best offensives had been stopped, and Lee never again threatened northern territory.

In 1864, the Vermonters again showed that they were skilled soldiers. In a thick forest in Virginia, known as The Wilderness, Lee was again gaining the upper hand. General Ulysses S. Grant sent in the 16th Corps, which included the Vermont Brigade. Facing terrible odds and suffering an extremely high death count, the Vermont men held until reinforcements arrived.

While the Vermont Brigade was gaining fame in the South, one battle was fought on Vermont soil. This northernmost battle of the war was fought in St. Albans. A group of Confederate soldiers had escaped from northern prisons into Canada. They knew Lee's army was in trouble and needed money for supplies. On October 19, 1864, a group of twenty men crossed the border to rob St. Albans's banks. They came in small groups disguised as tourists, businessmen, and invalids seeking cures.

At the proper time, they dropped their disguises and raided the three banks along Main Street. Some of them stayed outside rounding up frightened people in the park so they could not alert the hundreds of men working in the machine and railroad shops around the corner on Lake Street. Their bags bulging with money, the raiders stole horses to make their getaway. In the gunfight that broke out as they galloped away, many people were wounded, including one raider. One St. Albans man died of his wounds.

The Confederates raced out of town with $208,000 and a posse of Green Mountain Cavalry hot on their trail. They were able to cross the border into Canada before the cavalry could catch up. The U.S. troops had to obtain permission from the Canadian authorities to follow them into the country. By that time, the raiders had scattered and divided the money. Nevertheless, the Vermonters found fourteen of them and recovered $88,000.

The St. Albans raid of 1864. The raiders are demanding money from a teller in the St. Albans Bank. (Courtesy Vermont Historical Society)

Note

"To extradite" means to turn over criminals to another state or country.

They were near the U.S. border when Canadian police claimed the prisoners, carting them away to jail in Montreal. The United States went to court to force the Canadians to extradite the raiders. At the end of the trial, the Canadian judge gave the St. Albans raiders their freedom and the money. He said they had a right to attack the United States because they were in a state of war. The raiders returned to their home state of Kentucky and were welcomed as heroes for their daring robbery of three Vermont banks.

The money was not enough to help the South to victory. In 1865, Lee surrendered at Appomattox Court House in Virginia. That December, the Thirteenth Amendment to the Constitution was passed abolishing slavery. Vermont had played an important part in destroying this shameful institution.

The Suffrage Movement

Some people believed that freedom from slavery also meant freeing women from their slavery. Rachael and Rowland T. Robinson, the Underground Railroad conductors mentioned earlier, were two supporters of women's rights. They fought to have women admitted into the Vermont Anti-Slavery Society in 1840. At about the same time, Clarina H. Nichols, a newspaper editor, began speaking out for women's rights. This seems to be the beginning of the suffrage movement in Vermont.

Note

Suffrage is the right to vote.

Some women had thought about their lot in life before the mid-1800s, but they simply had had no time to do anything about it. Women's work on the farm seemed never-ending. Even with machines taking over many of the chores that women used to do, many needed to leave the home to work ten to thirteen hours a day in factories. When they came home, they cooked, cleaned, and otherwise took care of the family.

In those families where the husbands supported their goals, women had more time to fight for their rights.

"What rights didn't they have?" you might ask. Under the law, women were the property of their husbands. They were not allowed to inherit property; they had to hand over any wages to their husbands; and they were not allowed to use the banks. Men believed that since women could not vote, there was no reason to educate them beyond elementary school. Despite this, a few women did manage to get a secondary school education. They were not, however, allowed to enter Vermont's colleges or three medical schools. If a woman did receive a medical degree in another state, she was not allowed to practice medicine in Vermont's hospitals. No matter how cruel her husband was, if a woman left him, she was not allowed to take her children with her. The list of restrictions goes on and on.

Slowly, women in Vermont began to join together to fight for their rights. They fought for equal pay and employment, property and education rights, and the right to vote. The most active spokeswoman in the state was Clarina Howard Nichols, born in Townshend in 1810. Her family was well-to-do and believed in education for women. After her schooling, she married a man who turned out to be a very cruel husband. She worked at the marriage for nine years but finally left him.

Because she was an educated woman, she found a job working as a journalist on the Brattleboro *Democrat*. She married the editor, George Nichols, and in the 1840s, he put her in charge of the paper. At first she kept it a secret because she was afraid that people would not accept a woman editor. But she soon proved she was capable, and circulation increased. She used the editorial page to print antislavery and prosuffrage articles. Through her paper, she drummed up a great deal of support for the argument that women should have the right to own property. Partly because of Clarina Nichols, Vermont became the first state to give women increased property rights in 1847.

Clarina Nichols was proud of her state, but she moved slowly. Next she tackled

The Lowell Offering *was written by factory girls in the mills of Lowell, Massachusetts, between 1820 and 1850. It was the first magazine in the United States written solely by women. Its coeditor, Harriot Curtis, was one of the thousands of Vermonters who moved south to work in the mills. "[W]e could never understand," she wrote, "why a man's time and service were, in fact, more valuable than women's when the labor was equally as well performed by one as the other." Not until 1963 was the Equal Pay Act for men and women passed. Many inequities still exist. (Sophia Smith Collection, Smith College)*

women's right to vote at school meetings. The Vermont legislature invited her to speak to them on the issue. She became the first woman to address the general assembly in December 1852. Although she was nervous, she gave an eloquent speech in favor of women's rights. Despite this, the men of the legislature voted down the petition.

She continued to fight for women's rights, but two years later, she left Vermont, discouraged. She and her family moved to Kansas to help prevent it from becoming a slave state. There, she had more luck changing the laws against women. She gained a national reputation while succeeding in getting many rights for women included in the Kansas constitution.

Not until 1880 did Vermont women finally win the right to vote at school meetings. Their next goal was voting at town meetings. Six times between 1888 and 1917, the legislature voted on that issue, and each time the men turned it down. What would you do if you lost six times? Vermont women continued to fight!

Leaders of the movement urged women to refuse to pay their taxes if they had no say in how they were spent. Miss Daniels of Grafton, who owned quite a lot of property, refused to pay when the tax collector came around in 1910. Town officials did not know what to do. It caused quite a stir, as you can imagine, and more people than ever before started discussing the suffrage issue.

Finally, in 1917, Vermont became the first New England state to allow women to vote at town meetings. In many states farther west, women were already voting in town, state, and even federal elections. In 1919, the Vermont legislature passed a bill giving women full voting rights, but Governor Percival Clement refused to sign it. Vermont women had to wait until 1920, when the Nineteenth Amendment to the U.S. Constitution gave women the right to vote. They wasted no time. The next year, the residents of Orange County sent the first Vermont woman, Edna L. Beard, to the state legislature to represent them.

The fight for equality was far from over. Just because women could vote did not mean the discrimination stopped. They were allowed to hold only the lowest paying jobs, and even if a woman was doing the exact same job as a man, she was paid less. Today, despite even more advances in women's rights, most women still earn less than most men.

Education

Through education, men had many more opportunities than women. Vermonters had long believed in the importance of education for their sons. The original town charters of the eighteenth century set aside a plot of land for schools. Vermont was one of the first to charter a state university in 1791. The University of Vermont opened its doors to men in 1800. (Women were allowed to attend seventy-two years later.) Also in 1800, the first U.S. academy for the training of women opened in Middlebury. It did not train women for professional jobs but provided training in skills needed to take care of the home. In 1819, Vermont opened the nation's first private military college, later named Norwich University. The first U.S. normal school for training teachers was started in 1823 at Concord Corner. That is quite a few firsts for one state.

The state required each town to provide a school for its children. Even though many towns were poor and could not afford much, they made sure they had at least one room and one teacher. The one-room schoolhouse often was cold, overcrowded, and uncomfortable, and the teacher frequently had no training. The towns hired peddlers, college students, and businessmen as teachers, but there never seemed to be enough to go around. Soon the towns turned to women to help relieve the teacher shortage. By the 1850s, seventy percent of Vermont's teachers were women.

Living conditions for teachers were not always pleasant. They received a room and meals at a different student's house each week. Most families did not have big houses, and the teachers usually had to sleep in the same room as their students. Women received five dollars a month salary; men received fifteen.

Handling all the classroom duties also was difficult. Some teachers had as many as eighty to one hundred students. Discipline often became the most important subject taught. Any sort of punishment was all right as long as there was no permanent injury. Teachers often feruled students who misbehaved or had not learned their lessons. Using a birch switch on bare legs was another method of discipline. Many an unhappy student found himself in the corner with a dunce cap on his head or a "lazy" sign hung around his neck.

Note

"To ferule" means to hit with a ruler or other flat piece of wood.

In 1859, a baby born in Burlington would grow up to fight to change these cruel methods of discipline. His name was John Dewey. He went to school in Burlington as a boy and there learned to hate the whippings that students endured. Later he attended the University of Vermont and Johns Hopkins University in Maryland. After studying hard and talking to other people about the education of his time, Dewey came up with some new educational ideas.

He said that using physical force on students was wrong. They should not be whipped or ridiculed. He also thought that teachers should not dictate to their students *what* to think but should teach them *how* to think. He began to travel a great deal to teach others about his ideas. His fame spread around the world during the early part of the twentieth century. He wrote books about his new school of thought, and these were translated into many languages, from Spanish to Arabic to Chinese. Many students around the world probably are happier because of John Dewey.

Despite what seemed like a cruel system of educating their youth, Vermont schoolteachers were eagerly sought in the West. This new job market gave women a freedom they had never known. While many families were crossing the prairie to find farmland, single women were making the journey to teach. Cynthia Bishop from Georgia, Vermont, wrote home from New Durham, Indiana, in 1853: "I had the offer of two schools, one of which I could not refuse if I tried. They were so (pressing) in their application. . . I was amused by their confidence that they would have a good school if they obtained my services. . . ."*

The Environment

One giant to come out of Vermont in the nineteenth century was George Perkins Marsh (1801–1882). He grew up in Woodstock on the lower slopes of Mount Tom. He is generally considered the first American to question the wholesale stripping of the forests. Of course, the Native Americans had long watched and mourned what the whites were doing to their land. They knew that peace with nature was essential to life on this earth. The white people did not begin to learn that lesson until the nineteenth century, and it was George P. Marsh who opened the eyes of Americans to the destruction around them.

*Polly W. Kaufman, *Women Teachers on the Frontier* (New Haven, Conn.: Yale University, 1984), p. 171.

Over his lifetime of eighty-one years, Marsh observed immense change taking place in our state. As a boy, he remembered lush forests and abundant wildlife. He witnessed the gradual stripping of the trees from the land for potash or lumber and the disappearance of the wildlife. As a young farmer, he also participated in this destruction of the environment. But he was always watching and thinking about what was going on around him. As he grew older, he began to see what was happening. He remembered that when he was a boy, the rain used to seep into the forest soil and slowly feed the streams and the Ottauquechee River near his home. As a man, he saw the water running rapidly down the bare slopes and causing more floods than anyone could remember.

While other people wondered how nature could be so cruel, Marsh looked for answers. In 1847, he was invited to the

George Perkins Marsh was the first to speak out against the damage done by wholesale stripping of the forests. He is considered the first environmentalist. (Special Collection University of Vermont Library)

Rutland Fair to judge pigs and oxen and to speak to the Agricultural Society of Rutland County. It was there that he first proposed an answer to the problems plaguing the land.

"There is reason to fear," he said, "that the valleys of many of our streams will soon be converted from smiling meadows into broad wastes of shingle and gravel and pebbles, deserts in summer and seas in autumn and spring." If people will not replant the cleared ground, then they should at least leave nature alone to reclothe her bare hills "with a spontaneous growth of wood."* But reforestation was a new idea, and people did not take to it right away.

Seventeen years later, Marsh published his thoughts on the environment in a book called *Man and Nature; or Physical Geography as Modified by Human Action*. His ideas about conserving nature and replanting the forests did not take hold immediately. Vermonters continued to chop away at their forest heritage until they reached a low point at the turn of the century, when only one-quarter of the state still had trees.

Reforestation had begun naturally in some places as the hill farms were abandoned, and some people began to take Marsh's ideas seriously. A man named Frederick Billings bought the old Marsh farm and became a pioneer in replanting the hills. Today, the old homestead is a working dairy farm and museum, preserving the environment and Vermont's heritage. George Perkins Marsh would no doubt be proud of how his boyhood home is being used today.

Marsh accomplished many other things in his life. He learned to speak twenty

*"Address Delivered Before the Agricultural Society of Rutland County," quoted in Charles T. Morrissey, *Vermont, A History* (New York: W. W. Norton and Company, 1984), p. 187.

languages, built roads, quarried marble, and made tools. He became a lawyer, teacher, congressman, and world diplomat. He spent five years in Turkey and twenty-one in Italy as a U.S. ambassador. But he remained a down-to-earth Vermonter. He believed in equality among people and never thought that his works put him above anyone else.

Today, Vermonters are carrying on the tradition started by George Perkins Marsh. Environmental concerns are taken into account whenever we need more land for housing or people need more room for their businesses. All the rules are spelled out in Act 250, which we will explore in Section III.

In this unit, we have met only a few of the Vermonters who influenced our nation. There were many more. Henry Wells of Thetford was one half of Wells, Fargo, a famous transportation system begun in California. Frederick Billings of Woodstock was the prime mover in building the Northern Pacific Railroad. William Wilson of East Dorset and Robert Smith of St. Johnsbury formed Alcoholics Anonymous. Two Pawlet men, Philo P. Stewart and John J. Shepherd, founded Oberlin College in Ohio. It was the first U.S. college to admit women and blacks.

Ex-Vermonters were powerful in politics, too. In 1880, every powerful Republican in Wisconsin had been born in Vermont. Between 1850 and 1900, eighty-eight native Vermonters represented other states in Congress. No other state in the union had such a large percentage of native sons making the laws for our country. Today, the people of our state continue to influence the nation on various issues. Can you think of what they are before you read about them in the next section?

Story

Note

Ciphering is the solving of problems by means of arithmetic.

Winter Term at a Vermont School (1830)

John Olmstead approached the district school standing on a bleak and lonely stretch of land outside of town. He wondered if he had made the right decision. He needed money for law school, true, but would he be able to handle the fifty children who would soon be seated in this small wooden building? The school had closed down last year because the mutinous children had "put out" three masters.

Since it was such a hard school, he had been offered higher wages than usual—twenty dollars a month instead of the usual fifteen. The committeemen had taken one look at his six-foot frame, established that he attended church every Sunday and could cipher, and hired him immediately to keep the "savages" in line.

Olmstead was of the new school of thought that children were not born evil but were created neutral. He decided to try reasoning with the ruffians but keep the rod handy just in case.

Entering the building, he looked around the room and hoped that everything was ready for his first day of school. Backless benches lined the walls, and slates were stacked at the end of each bench. The children would bring their own family books—Noah Webster's *The Elementary Spelling-book*, known as *The Old Blue-back*, and a copy of the Old Testament. He had recently bought Jedidiah Morse's *Geography Made Easy* and intended to have the children memorize from it. He felt that they needed to know more about the world now that the United States was expanding. He soon had a fire roaring in the stove, the centerpiece of the room.

Before long, the master heard noises outside and went to the door to welcome the children. "The master is already here," someone yelled.

"Wonder how long this 'n 'll last."

John Olmstead took a deep breath and bade the children to sit—boys on one side, girls on the other. When they were seated, he introduced himself and asked an older boy to read from the Old Testament. During the reading, he heard something rolling around the floor. Walking to the back, he saw two boys playing marbles. He bent down, took the marbles, and started to walk away.

As he did, he heard a rough voice say, "Master Olmstead, you ought'n to behave that way. Them's my marbles." He whirled around to identify the speaker, a boy named Lewis. Olmstead was amazed that anyone would interrupt the reading of the Old Testament. "Stop reading," he demanded sharply. "Young man," he said looking right at Lewis, "you are not to yell out—we are reading the Lord's book."

"I don't care, I want my marbles." Snickers and giggles were heard around the room.

Olmstead was not prepared for such boldness. His mouth went dry; he tried to swallow. Finally, he stalked over to Lewis, picked him up, and sat him on the bench farthest from the fire. Looking him in the eyes, he said, "I hadn't intended to use the rod, but you'll be the first one to feel it if I hear one more word out of your mouth." That seemed to quiet the group, for a while anyway.

After the Old Testament reading, he asked the scholars to copy a page from the speller into their notebooks. One at a time, they brought their notebooks up to his desk so he could check their writing. The notebooks were made out of rough, dark paper. Each piece was folded to make eight pages, then put together to make the proper thickness. A brown paper cover was added and sewed up the middle. The children had ruled them themselves.

During this time, Olmstead started to learn their names. "Mornin' Master, my name's Charity," said one black-eyed girl. Whispering, she added, "Lewis took my seat, sir. Must I sit back in the cold?"

Jumping up, he saw everyone watching him intently. Lewis looked at him from under his ragged brown hair with a mocking scowl. Olmstead felt the anger reddening his face. *So you don't think I'd dare use the rod*, he thought. He grabbed the rod, walked over to Lewis, and whipped him soundly on the shins. "Get to your own seat and mind your work," he cried. Lewis sulked to the back of the room.

Returning to his desk, John Olmstead was still angry. *Could it be true that reasoning doesn't work with children?* he wondered. No, he was determined to try it again when he had a chance.

During the rest of the morning, the children read sentences from the speller or primer (whichever they had brought from home) and recited spelling words in groups. Olmstead managed to collect ten more marbles, two balls, and five penknives, which he deposited in his desk. He was relieved to send them home for lunch.

Will I survive twelve weeks of this? he wondered as he returned to the family's home where he was boarding for the week for lunch. The hour flew by, and he grudgingly returned to the schoolhouse, but he saw no children.

That's odd, he thought. *Perhaps I'm early*. Trying the door, he found that it would not open. Laughter and pandemonium broke loose within. "Ha! Now we'll have a fine time all afternoon," someone yelled.

"Yeah, we've gotten our things from your desk, too."

Oh, no! Olmstead thought. *I've been barred out. I can't let them get the best of me.*

He could not reason with them because it was too noisy inside. Suddenly, an idea came to him. He climbed the old oak next to the school, jumped on the roof, and covered the chimney flue with his coat. Soon he heard coughing, and fifty children came tumbling out of the building. As soon as the choking subsided, Olmstead cried from the roof, "Now go inside, put your toys back in my desk, and be seated." The children obeyed him. He breathed a sigh of relief.

The afternoon went relatively smoothly after that. There was more reading and spelling—out loud of course. Working silently was practically unheard of. The final hour was spent ciphering. The master read rules and problems, and the scholars copied them into their notebooks.

Finally, he dismissed the children, saying, "Go straight home and be civil to everybody you may meet." After they had all left, he sat down on a bench and thought that he had never been so tired and tense in his whole life. How much more could he take?

After a while, he headed back toward his house for the first week. He walked the long way, by the forest, to help himself unwind. Occasionally, he thought he saw movement through the trees and became nervous. Indians were said to lurk along the road. He thought of the stories in the reading lessons, and the gruesome details of Indian cruelty loomed large in the settling dusk.

Going farther, he came upon a small log house on the edge of the forest. Two large black eyes stared at him from around the corner, but they belonged to such a tiny little boy that he lost much of his nervousness.

"Hi, what's your name?"

The child ran into the house. Immediately, an Indian woman appeared. She said nothing—just stared at him with hollow eyes.

"I'm sorry, I didn't mean to scare him. I'm the new schoolmaster on my way home. The quietness of the forest seemed soothing."

"That's a strange thing for a white man to say," she finally answered. "You have destroyed most of the forest and come to what is left for calmness. The troubled spirits that dwell here have none to share."

She looked so lonely. He wanted to find out more about her. "Are you alone here with your children?"

"My husband is out hunting. There is little game left. He will stay out till he kills something."

"Perhaps if you moved out west—the game is plentiful there they say."

For the first time, emotion flashed in her eyes. "You have stolen everything from us—our land, our ancient rights, even our bodies must dwell in your world. But our minds and souls belong here on our traditional lands. The roots of our being are here. Here we are one with our ancestors, close to their souls. You have taken everything, but you will not take our souls."

John Olmstead began to feel very uncomfortable. A vague feeling of guilt enveloped him, and he had to escape back to his own world. He ran toward the town, looking back once. A terrible loneliness seemed to surround the little cabin. He hurried home to his dinner.

He ate his mutton and drank his beer but could not shake the strange feeling the encounter with the Indian woman had given him. He decided to go to the public house for some company.

It was completely dark now as he headed to the tavern on the main street. The windows threw long yellow beams of light out onto the road, and he heard laughter from inside. Upon entering, he went straight to the bar. "How fare you? What have you got that's good to drink?"

"I have gin, West India and genuine New England, whiskey, and cider brandy," the landlord replied.

"I'll have a mug of your New England sweetened with molasses."

"Hey, schoolmaster, come an' set with us," someone yelled from the corner table.

He looked around and recognized one of the committeemen who had hired him. When he got his drink, he joined the men.

After the introductions, Hinkley said, "I hear you had a wee bit of trouble today with the scholars." Everyone laughed.

Before Olmstead could answer, Sawyer slapped him on the back and said, "You're a good man, Master Olmstead, handled 'em well. Gotta be strict, or they'll run you out like the rest. They're a bunch of savages sometimes."

"Talking of savages," Hinkley said, "hear about this new law Congress passed? Indian Removal Act they call it. Gonna take all those filthy barbarians and move 'em west of the Mississippi."

"Could move 'em all the way to the Pacific and drop 'em in for all I care," Parley said. "I'm afraid to walk the roads at night—them's always lurking in the trees waiting to attack God-fearing people."

Everyone murmured agreement. John Olmstead could not move. A weight began to grow in his stomach. He thought back to the isolated cabin and to the Indian woman. *So we've taken your soul after all.* He was in no mood to stay and took his leave. He walked home under the starless sky, wondering about his world. That night, he could not sleep. His brain was exploding with so many questions about school and how to treat children, about the Indian woman and what her family would do now. What was right? Would he ever find the answers?

SECTION III

20th-Century Issues

UNIT 9

Hard Times

The twentieth century started out quite differently from the nineteenth. Just after achieving statehood, Vermont's population was doubling and tripling, and business was booming. By the 1900s, however, Vermont life had slowed down considerably. Much of the soil had worn out. Newcomers were not streaming to the state to farm. Production in industry had leveled off. Laborers were still needed but not in as great a number as before. Many of Vermont's people again migrated out of the state to earn a living. During two decades (1910 and 1930), Vermont actually lost population for the first time in its history.

The first half of the twentieth century seemed to be one sacrifice after another. In 1917, the United States joined with Europeans in their war against Germany. During this first World War, more than sixteen thousand Vermont men and women served in Europe; 642 lost their lives, and 886 were wounded. Many others died from a 1919 influenza epidemic that swept Europe and the United States.

Nine years after the end of the war, after people had put their lives back together, a terrible disaster struck Vermont. In 1927, a great flood washed over the state. Many people died, and the water caused millions of dollars worth of damage. As the state was recovering from the flood, the Depression hit in 1929. Businesses were ruined; thousands of people were out of work; life savings disappeared as banks collapsed. Many lives were destroyed all across the country. No matter where you moved, the story was the same. For the first time in the history of our country, more people left the country than immigrated here.

As the country and the state began to recover from the Depression, another World War began in Europe (1939). The United States entered the war in 1941, and thousands of Vermonters enlisted in the armed forces. Many other men and women stayed home to work the farms and raise food for civilians and soldiers. Vermont's textile and machine industries again began to hum with activity for the war effort.

After the war, the hard times slowly came to an end. By the 1950s, the bitter struggles seemed to be over, and Vermonters were ready for better times ahead. But before we get to the good times, let's see what it was like to live through the Great Flood of 1927 and the Great Depression.

The Great Flood of 1927

The autumn of 1927 was a very wet one for New England. By November, the hills and valleys in Vermont were soaked with water; the ground could hold no more. Then on November 3 and 4, severe rainstorms hit the state. Unable to hold more water, the rivers became torrents overflowing their banks and destroying homes, industries, farms, bridges, and roads. Eighty-five people drowned, including Lieutenant Governor Hollister

In the Great Flood of 1927, 4 lives were lost in Barre. Others were rescued by people throwing ropes from the top of the oil tanks (left) on Webster Avenue. (Courtesy Vermont Historical Society)

Jackson. Before a special session of the general assembly, Governor John Weeks called it the "greatest catastrophe in Vermont's history."

It may well have been the worst natural disaster ever to hit the state. In its aftermath, many people were left homeless; cows, horses, and other livestock lay dead in the fields; and travel was almost at a standstill. Roads, bridges, and railroad tracks had been washed out by the roaring waters. Vermont needed $8.5 million to repair the damage. Where would the money come from?

Vermonters had a pay-as-you-go attitude toward life, and they did not like the idea of borrowing money. If they did not have the money on hand, they went without. But this was an emergency; repairs could not wait. The first thing they did was turn to each other. That was not unusual; Vermonters had been doing that for years. Farmers helped each other at barn raisings; the Green Mountain Boys had protected land rights; laborers acted together for better wages. But this time they reached out a little farther, and that stretching out of the hand had far-reaching effects on Vermont's future.

First, the state legislature decided to borrow money by selling bonds. (Bonds are certificates that citizens buy with the promise to repay holders on a specified date in the future. The holders of the bonds also receive interest on their money.) Second, the governor asked for and received $2.6 million from the federal government. It was almost like asking a neighbor for help, since Calvin Coolidge of Plymouth, Vermont, was president at the time. That federal money went a long way toward helping to rebuild Vermont's roads and bridges.

The legislature decided to take the responsibility for roads out of the hands of the counties. (It had been taken out of the hands of the towns in 1880, when farmers had wanted better roads to get their goods to market.) With a mixture of state and federal funding, Vermont built a system of hardtop roads that became the state highway system still in place today. For the first time Vermonters had good, hard roads running the length and breadth of the state.

The establishment of this road system is important for several reasons. First, state government became a little more powerful in the effort to help all Vermonters. The state had long been helping farmers by regulating dairy and railroad prices and was helping small towns with school costs. But now the state began selling bonds and running the road system. The state passed its first income tax law in 1931 to raise money to maintain the roads. This tax was passed during the Great Depression, so you can imagine how unpopular it was.

Second, this was the first sign that Vermonters were willing to ask for help from the federal government. They realized that "rugged individualism" was not the only choice. Sometimes people need help from other sources, and they should not be afraid to ask.

The roads paved the way for a few more changes in Vermont. The early twentieth century was the beginning of the automobile age in our country. In 1920, the United States had nine million registered cars; by 1930, there were thirty million. With Vermont's improved road system, more and more cars were motoring through the state by the end of the

President Calvin Coolidge of Plymouth Notch is shown working on his farm. He was our 30th president, serving from 1923 to 1929. (Special Collections University of Vermont Library)

decade. Workers no longer needed to live near their work but instead could live outside the cities and commute. Farmers could leave their isolated farms and travel to neighboring cities more frequently. The rural and urban areas drew a little closer together.

More and more people took to the road to see Vermont, and Vermonters drove to other parts of the country. Lifestyles mixed, and people began to understand the differences among various parts of the country. Some of the differences even began to disappear as people of different regions borrowed ideas from each other. As you can see, the Great Flood of 1927 changed Vermont in more ways than anyone could have foreseen.

The Great Depression

Another event that had a long-lasting effect on Vermont was the Great Depression, which began in 1929. For a variety of reasons, businesses began to collapse all over the country. Thousands of Vermont workers were laid off, with no way of receiving money. (There were no unemployment or welfare checks in those days.) Those who still had jobs had their wages cut drastically. Many banks were forced to close their doors, and people lost every cent they had saved. As people had less money to buy things, more companies went out of business and more workers lost their jobs. It was a horrible time for people all over the country. Just finding enough to eat became a monumental task for many.

Some say that rural Vermonters did not suffer quite as much as city folks. They could turn to gardening, fishing, and hunting to help feed their families. But Vermont did not have the plentiful game of its early days; sometimes one pigeon would have to make do for the family meal. Many people were hungry all the time—not the kind of hunger you feel just before lunch, but a continual empty gnawing in the pit of your stomach, day after day.

Just as in the months after the Great Flood of 1927, people could not make it on their own. They needed help from each other and from the state and federal governments. The state put people to work on the new state highway system and helped farmers market and control prices of their dairy products. By 1931, all but two of Vermont's creameries had joined New England Dairies, Inc. (To this day, New England dairy farmers cooperate with each other to sell their products.) Since 1909, Vermont had been working on a plan to reforest the state and manage the forests to make sure that the hills were never stripped again. Some Vermonters were put to work thinning and pruning the forests to ensure healthy growth.

Vermont also received millions of dollars from the federal government to put people back to work. At first, many towns did not want the money because the federal government tried to tell them how to spend it. When given considerable freedom in deciding how to spend the money, however, Vermonters accepted the funds.

Vermont had already drawn up a flood control plan because of the Great Flood. The federal government provided the money to build a series of dams throughout the state to guard against future flooding. One of the more successful federal programs in Vermont was the Civilian Conservation Corps (CCC). The U.S. government recruited about three million unmarried men from across the country to do eight hours of conservation work a day. When they enrolled in the CCC, the men promised to accept assignment to any CCC camp in the country, keep the barracks and camp clean, and send a part of their pay to their families. The government gave them clothes, room, board, a salary, and thirty dollars a month for spending money.

When the CCC first began operating in March 1933, Vermont was allowed only four camps. Since the state already had conservation plans, Vermont opened one of the first camps in April in the state forest near Mount Tabor. Vermont soon exceeded her limit for camps, and by 1934, the state had eighteen CCC camps; by 1937, it had thirty.

More than forty thousand young men from Vermont and other states worked together replanting our forests, building more than one hundred miles of roads, controlling insects and disease, and preventing forest fires. They also worked on flood control and soil erosion projects and built recreational roads and trails. They improved animal habitats and rural school buildings and reclaimed abandoned farms.

One of the more far-reaching projects was designing and cutting trails for Vermont's ski areas. A large CCC camp was constructed at Moscow in Stowe. The young men built the first ski trails on Mount Mansfield, including the Bruce, the Ski Meister, and the Nose Dive. The CCC also began developing other ski areas around the state and helped put Vermont on the road to becoming the "Ski Capital of the East."

Civilian Conservation Corps (CCC) workers chop trees on Mount Mansfield during the Depression. (Courtesy Vermont Historical Society)

Living in a CCC Camp

Life was not easy for these young men (between age eighteen and age twenty-five), who left their families and homes to live in barracks in rural areas for six months to two years. They had to adjust to a whole new way of life in a military-like atmosphere. But at least they had jobs and something to eat.

One of Vermont's camps was Camp William James at Sharon. The project there was to reclaim abandoned farms in the area and prepare them for resettlement. Two young men kept journals describing life at the camp. The following quotes are from their journals, written during the winter of 1941. Let's look over the shoulders of Hodding and Page Smith as they write about life at Camp William James.*

January 18: The square dance this evening was an almost incredible success. Ed Larkin, of Tunbridge, was one caller, and the other was the Rev. Fisk, from Hanover, who brought along records and an amplifying set. Girls came from Springfield, Vermont, as well as from Hanover, Norwich, Tunbridge, etc.

This whole affair is unprecedented in the CCC. For the first time since they enrolled, these fellows saw some real hearty fun and life. I felt, personally, that it was a little too early in Camp to do this. As yet we had done nothing, and so deserved nothing. But it was such a terrific success.

January 20: Frank, Jack, Al and I drove to Four Wells. They felt very low, and got very silly, trying to buck up each other with jokes about serious things.

January 23: Eugen and Mr. Amos went over to Brocklebank (abandoned farm) yesterday. O'Brien said he is now worried about the feasibility of the project since the land is weak and unproductive. But if we don't bring back the most remote place and connect it up with the community again, we will never succeed.

February 6: O.B. Stollard loafed all day—chews tobacco, swears. A real problem. He must be deprived of the pick-up.

Note

"Feasibility" means possibility or workability.

*From Jack J. Preiss, *Camp William James* (Norwich, Vermont: Argo Books, 1978), pp. 121–135.

Fremont Smith was up in arms this morning about the towns. He bawled out the woman in the Sharon store for the way people in the town were gossiping, and believing the newspaper stories, and not cooperating with the Camp. He wants to go to every one of the nine townships as soon as possible and explain to the people what we're aiming to do. He's wonderful.

February 10: We need a lot more exercise and sport, loud laughter, and vigor. Farming doesn't appeal to boys today. It's not the long hours, but the loneliness and emptiness of the land that hurts. Only groups of people can settle an area. Isolation is ruinous.

We need to find a place for quiet talks, where people can go in pairs and small groups. Life in the barracks is too public.

February 18: Stanley Flint and I saw a number of farmers in Tunbridge, Chelsea, and Vershire on the possibility of cutting wood on shares on their land. Farmers feel this is the best thing that the government had done yet. It enables the Camp to serve its real function in regard to the labor supply. Some fellows don't like the project because it smacks of charity to the farmers, who get all the benefit free. But there is no other project at the moment.

Frank told me of the brilliant job Mogan and Winces had done in trying to convince Jones to stay in Camp. They told Jones that if he left he'd go back to being the hired hand that he hated to be. They agreed that a lot of Vermont farmers were dumb and lazy, and that Jones shouldn't have to work for them.

As you can see, there was much tension in the camps, both among the CCC workers and between the workers and the townspeople. Some of the men in the camps were from cities and did not understand the rural way of life. Despite such difficulties, people managed to work together and complete many important jobs for the good of our state.

Labor During the Depression

It was relatively easy to pass legislation to help out the farmers because they always had a majority in the state house of representatives (see Unit 11). But while they were joining together to pass legislation and young men were working together in CCC camps, men and women in industry were struggling to make a living. As we discussed in Unit 7, many workers had joined unions to negotiate with the owners or managers of their companies. It was a new idea for owners, who were used to treating workers as the owners thought best. The owners had always set wages with no interference from the workers. Now the workers wanted a say in determining their wages and working conditions. The owners did not want to give up that power to the workers. The stage was set for many serious struggles.

One of the worst struggles occurred in Bellows Falls. It had been a "paper town" for more than one hundred years, and many men and women made a living in the paper industry there. In 1921, the International Paper Company wanted to cut wages by thirty percent. The unionized workers wanted to negotiate, but the company refused. Four hundred people went on strike, and the company hired other workers to take their place.

The company went to court to stop the workers from picketing the plant. At that time, there were no laws protecting the rights of workers to bargain collectively and to strike. The courts forbade the workers to assemble or picket. Four years later, the company moved to Canada, never having negotiated with the workers.

Another company that refused to negotiate with its workers was the Vermont Marble Company in Proctor, still run by the Proctor family at that time. The Proctors believed that they should determine wages based on costs, sales, and other conditions in the industry. The owners knew what was best, they said. The Proctors provided the workers with company housing, fuel, and electricity. Payment for these was taken out of the workers' wages, which amounted to only about twelve dollars a week during the Depression. Many believed that these were starvation wages and that the company could afford more.

In 1935, unionized marbleworkers demanded a raise. The company refused to discuss it, and in February, nearly one thousand workers went on strike. The company then sent notices to many families evicting them from the company houses. Many people felt that the owner was inhumane in his treatment of the workers. *Nation* magazine demanded to know, "Who are these Proctors of Proctor who take no reasonable steps to conciliate and now deliver eviction notices to 186 families?"*

Note

"To conciliate" means to make peace.

Many of the townspeople, however, sided with the Proctors. Local police and townspeople broke the ranks of the strikers with beatings and arrests. Machine guns were used to threaten the strikers. The suffering of the workers continued for months. Despair grew as families had little food or clothing. Children had no milk to drink.

Gradually, many workers returned to the quarries at the same wages. Several hundred continued the strike until July 1936, but they could not afford to hold out forever and finally returned to work with no raise. They had been beaten by a company that refused to discuss wages with its workers and a town that would not support them.

A strikingly different atmosphere surrounded labor struggles in Barre, considered the capital of organized labor in Vermont. During the Depression (1932), the workers in the granite quarries had accepted a cut in wages due to the hard times. But when the company asked for a three dollar per day cut the next year, the workers refused. In April, about three thousand workers went on strike. The company hired replacements and asked the governor to send in the National Guard. The community was outraged; farmers, churchmen, even the American Legion protested the presence of the National Guard in their town.

As the strike wore on, local farmers and tradesmen gave food to the striking workers and asked the company to negotiate. Finally, the company agreed to sit down at the bargaining table with the union. Soon the strike was over. It had lasted two months as opposed to eighteen months in Proctor. The workers returned to work with a one dollar a day cut instead of the three dollars originally proposed. Negotiations and community support proved that people could work together to settle their differences.

In 1937, George Aiken became the governor of Vermont. He brought a more friendly attitude toward labor to the State House. "Labor in Vermont," he said, "should . . . have as favorable working conditions as in the states about us. We should not become a haven for industries employing underpaid and underprivileged labor."†

---

*Anita Marlburg, "Struggle in Marble," *Nation*, 1 April 1936, p. 414. Quoted in Faith Learned Pepe, *Vermont Workers, Vermont Resources* (Brattleboro, Vermont: Brattleboro Museum and Art Center, 1984), p. 17.

†Richard M. Judd, *The New Deal in Vermont: Its Impact and Aftermath* (New York: Garland Publishing, 1979), p. 154.

By the 1940s, labor unions had come to Vermont to stay. Through the foundation laid by pioneers in the early part of this century, many workers and owners now negotiate peacefully concerning wages and working conditions. Many laws protect the rights of workers to unionize and bargain collectively. Negotiations occasionally still end in bitter strikes, but much progress has been made in relations between labor and management.

Shortly after the labor difficulties began to simmer down, the United States entered World War II. From 1941 to 1945, more than fifty thousand Vermonters fought in the war. Of those, more than twelve thousand lost their lives on foreign soil. Back home, people were working again as Vermont factories contributed to the war effort. The sacrifices of many men and women helped bring the war to a successful end in the summer of 1945.

That same year, the nations of the world decided to form an organization where people could discuss their problems peacefully instead of going to war. That organization is the United Nations, which has its headquarters in New York City. Vermonter Warren Austin became the United States' first ambassador to the United Nations. He served for many years and sat through numerous debates among representatives of countries trying to work out their differences. When someone asked him if he became bored listening to so many speeches, he answered, "Yes, but it is better for aged diplomats to be bored than for young men to die."*

Gradually, life seemed to be getting better. During the 1950s, Vermont's population began to rise as new industries thrived and tourists motored to the Green Mountains. People were once again confident of earning a living in Vermont, and a renewed sense of pride emerged. From the 1960s to 1980s, the population has grown by leaps and bounds, mirroring this newfound prosperity and pride in being Vermonters.

Activity

> *Civilian Conservation Corps*
> (1, 2, 3, 18)
>
> Reread the February 6 entry in the CCC diary. Fremont Smith believed that the townspeople did not understand the purpose of the CCC. He wanted to explain it to them. What do you think the misunderstandings may have been? How would you describe the CCC to the people of Sharon, Vermont? Make a speech to give to the townspeople.

Activity

> *Diary*
> (1, 17, 19, 20)
>
> Reread the February 10 and 18 entries in the CCC diary. Do you see any contradictions? Do you think the writer understood the nature of rural life? Explain. Describe the stereotypes and/or prejudices in the entries. Are they fair? Do you think they exist in Vermont today? If you think they are unfair, what can be done to eliminate them?

*Dorothy Canfield Fisher, *Vermont Traditions* (Boston: Little, Brown and Company, 1953), p. 363.

UNIT 10

Vermonters at Work

History is not only in textbooks and in people's memories; it is happening all around you at this very moment. In fact, you are now a part of history. What you did yesterday and what you will do tomorrow is history in the making. Everyone in your classroom and in your family is making a contribution. For this reason, you will not have as many people and events to read about in these next two units; you will be able to search for historical happenings in the community around you.

Farmers in your area are still making difficult decisions about whether to sell their land or stay in an increasingly expensive business. Newcomers continue to come to Vermont as workers, tourists, and seekers of freedom. Others are fighting to save the environment from too much industry and overcrowding. The people of Vermont still oppose too many government controls over their lives.

Many of the activities in the rest of this book encourage you to take an active role in our history in the making by asking questions, identifying problems, seeking solutions, and making your own decisions about the future of your state. Not only will you be making history, but you also will be recording it for posterity. You will be twentieth-century historians.

Note
Posterity refers to future generations or descendants.

Earning a Living

One hundred years ago, almost half of all Vermonters worked in agriculture. Today, that number has shrunk to four percent. Farmers continually have retreated from the less fertile hill farms. Today's farms are on prime farmland and are much bigger than those of the past. Fewer farm hands are needed on modern farms because of technological improvements. The price of farmland has shot up because manufacturers, the recreation industry, and wealthy tourists are willing to spend a lot of money to buy prime land. Many farmers have not been able to afford the taxes on such valuable land, so they have sold out. For all these reasons, farming has ceased to be the most important way to earn a living in Vermont. Farming slipped out of the first spot in the 1940s and has been declining ever since.

How are Vermonters making a living today? The largest number of workers is in manufacturing. Most of them are making machinery, tools, or electronic equipment. The biggest names in this industry are IBM, Union Carbide, General Electric, Digital Equipment Corporation, and Johnson Controls.

The second largest group is working in the recreation industry or in services related to tourism. These services include motels, restaurants, ski-lift attendants, and service station employees. The major recreational activity is skiing in the Green Mountains at places such as Killington, Okemo, Stowe, and Jay Peak.

For whom are all these Vermonters working? All the major industries in the state are owned by people or corporations from other states. Vermonters have mixed feelings about this. On the one hand, these industries provide many jobs for Vermont residents. Wages in manufacturing are the best in the state. The companies pay high taxes, which help communities pay for many things they could not otherwise afford.

On the other hand, a large portion of the companies' profits are leaving the state. Those people working in recreation and tourism are the poorest paid workers. Since so many workers depend on tourism and recreation, Vermonters are only thirty-sixth in wages in the nation. Has Vermont become the "haven for industries employing underpaid...labor" that Governor George Aiken warned against?

Some workers are content with their wages; it is the trade-off they make for living in an uncrowded, clean environment. Others would like to develop Vermont into a state that pays higher wages, a state where there are enough jobs to go around. One way to do this, they say, is to promote tourism and small Vermont industries. As more tourists visited the state, more workers would be needed to serve them. More shops selling Vermont products and crafts could be opened. Farmland would have to be protected, as it is part of the scenery tourists come to see.

Others believe that promoting tourism is not enough. They argue that wages will stay low unless more manufacturing industries are brought to Vermont. They say we need to encourage out-of-state companies and those owned by Vermonters.

Many people believe a mixture of tourism and industry is the answer. Many heated discussions over the pros and cons of farming versus industry versus tourism echo throughout the hills and valleys of our state.

Environmental Issues

Promoting either industry or tourism causes concern among Vermonters—environmental concerns. Some industries pollute the water, air, and land. Too much development could strip the hills of their forests and cause damaging erosion as in the nineteenth century. An increased number of cars and trucks would bring chemicals that are harmful to plants, animals, and humans. More tourists and workers would mean more houses, hotels, and restaurants. What sort of energy resources should be used to run these homes and businesses?

Let's look at the tensions between development and the environment. One problem caused by increased development could be increased pollution from combustion, or burning. Study the illustration on the opposite page. As you can see, putting more chemicals and particles into the air is not good for plants or animals. One by-product is acid rain, which makes water and soil too acidic to support life. Buildings and metals corrode when exposed to this acid.

Currently, much of Vermont's acid rain comes from huge industries in the Midwest. Most Vermonters want to be very careful not to add to the problem. They want to make sure we have only clean, nonpolluting industries in the state.

Other problems that may accompany uncontrolled growth are erosion and water pollution. The ski industry is one example. Most Vermonters believe that the development of ski areas has been good for the state. They also believe that developers must be careful not to harm the environment. Cutting too many ski trails on the mountains can cause erosion, destruction of the mountain environment, and loss of wildlife habitat.

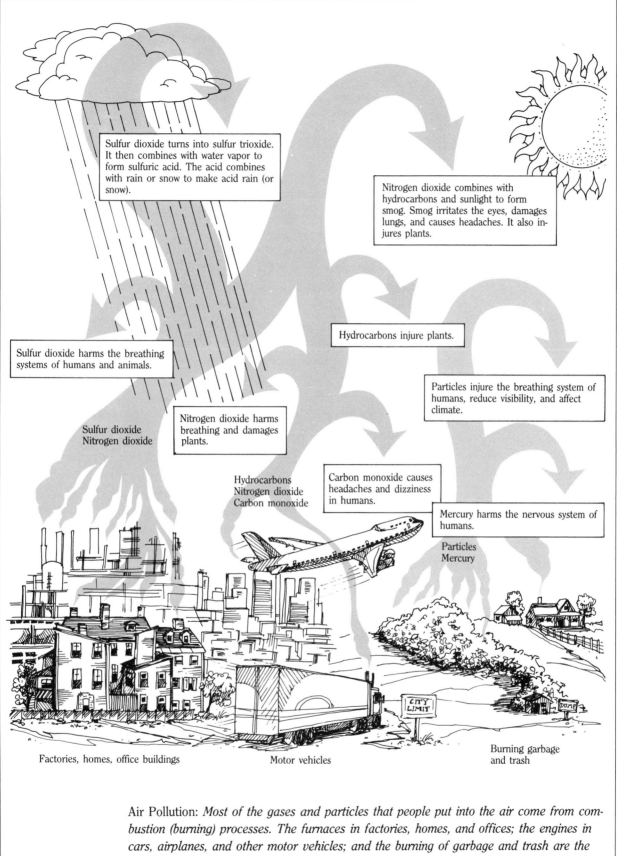

Sulfur dioxide turns into sulfur trioxide. It then combines with water vapor to form sulfuric acid. The acid combines with rain or snow to make acid rain (or snow).

Nitrogen dioxide combines with hydrocarbons and sunlight to form smog. Smog irritates the eyes, damages lungs, and causes headaches. It also injures plants.

Sulfur dioxide harms the breathing systems of humans and animals.

Hydrocarbons injure plants.

Particles injure the breathing system of humans, reduce visibility, and affect climate.

Sulfur dioxide
Nitrogen dioxide

Nitrogen dioxide harms breathing and damages plants.

Hydrocarbons
Nitrogen dioxide
Carbon monoxide

Carbon monoxide causes headaches and dizziness in humans.

Mercury harms the nervous system of humans.

Particles
Mercury

Factories, homes, office buildings

Motor vehicles

Burning garbage and trash

Air Pollution: *Most of the gases and particles that people put into the air come from combustion (burning) processes. The furnaces in factories, homes, and offices; the engines in cars, airplanes, and other motor vehicles; and the burning of garbage and trash are the chief sources of pollution from combustion. These pollutants have a wide variety of effects, as shown here.*

Similar destruction occurred in the past century, and Vermonters are eager to see that it does not happen again.

Condominiums near ski areas also need a place to discharge their waste materials. Developers say that the best way to handle the situation is to treat wastes and then spray them into the woods. The mountain soil will filter out any remaining harmful materials before the effluent (wastes) reaches any streams.

Environmentalists argue that the mountain soil is too thin and rocky to filter the effluent. In that case, sprayed wastes would harm mountain streams, kill aquatic life, and eventually reach the drinking systems of nearby communities. Scientists are divided on the issue, and more study is needed to determine who is right.

Because of these and other problems with development, Vermonters decided to control the unplanned use of the land. In the 1960s, they began talking about laws that would govern development and protect the environment. In 1970, the Vermont legislature, under the governorship of Deane C. Davis, passed a forward-looking law called Act 250. It was not meant to discourage development but to control it.

The law calls for land developers to plan before they build. To get a permit for development they must:

1. Plan for adequate water and sewage disposal.*
2. Make sure they do not cause pollution or erosion.
3. Not harm natural resources or historic sites.
4. Make sure roads can bear any increased traffic.
5. Make sure schools can absorb children if the population increases.

A plan must be presented before the district's environmental commission. Each commission has three members appointed by the governor. Since they have other jobs and work part-time on the commission, the members rely on the developers and "interested parties" in the community to provide them with the needed information to make a proper judgment. The active participation of citizens is important in this decision-making process.

As you can see, Vermonters struggle with some very important questions. We are challenged every day to come up with creative solutions to problems. How do we attract industry that will not harm our environment yet provides good-paying jobs for our citizens? How do we keep our tourist industry booming without causing overcrowded roads and resorts or damage to the environment? How do we protect our rural character while solving modern-day problems?

The answers to all these questions depend on how we view our state. What kinds of communities do we want to live in? We must answer these questions for ourselves and then work to implement the solutions. Vermonters have adapted to changes many times in the past; they will again.

Still They Come

No matter what kinds of problems we have in Vermont, people from all over the country and the world still find our state a wonderful place in which to live. Between 1960 and 1980, the population grew by more than thirty-one percent. The Green Mountains

---

*A 1985 water quality bill calls for permits for any sewage disposal.

beckon to people from other states and other countries. People from other states come to enjoy Vermont's rural character and small cities and towns. You know why people come from other countries: to escape poverty, wars, and persecution in their homeland. They search for freedom and jobs in a new country.

The newcomers continue to come from Europe, as they did in the past century, but more and more come from Central America and Asia. The largest increase in recent years has been among Hispanics from Mexico and Central America. In 1980, Vermont had more than three thousand new citizens of Spanish descent. More than one thousand blacks and as many Asians have recently found homes in the Green Mountains. New colors and customs once again add richness to our cultural patchwork.

Many newcomers face difficulties as they are confronted by the same sorts of problems the immigrants of the past century faced. They leave behind families and friends, along with familiar customs and languages. Many come from warm countries and must get used to our cold winters. They also face the prejudices of people who are uncomfortable with the differences among people.

Note

"To deport" means to send out of the country.

Some communities, such as Leicester, welcome newcomers. During the spring and summer of 1986, many Leicester citizens helped a Mexican family in their fight to stay in Vermont and become citizens. The U.S. Immigration Service said that they must return to Mexico. That decision "sparked an outpouring of support from their Leicester neighbors, who sponsored petition drives in an attempt to convince immigration officials not to deport the family."*

Vermont also welcomes people from other continents searching for freedom not found in their homeland. A family living near Guilford left Poland and settled in our state, which they say reminds them of their country. The father was a member of a labor union that was not allowed to protest poor working conditions. The mother is a concert violinist. Both have found greater freedom in Vermont. A famous Soviet writer, Aleksandr Solzhenitsyn, and his family came to Cavendish because of its rural character and the people's respect for individual privacy. He was not allowed to stay in the Soviet Union because his writings criticized the government.

Other families seek to escape death and persecution in war-torn countries. Many have come here from Southeast Asia, where the United States fought the Vietnam War during the 1960s and 1970s. (Many Vermonters fought in that war, and 138 died. Their names are carved on a monument on Route 89 in Sharon.) The United States pulled out of Vietnam in 1973, but the war did not end for the people of that and surrounding countries. As a result, many families are still in danger. Hundreds of Asian families have made Vermont their new home.

Vermont continues to be a place where people find freedom, peace, and opportunities. We have problems, but as in the nineteenth century, Vermonters stand ready to lend a helping hand to those searching for what we have found in the Green Mountain State.

---

*"Mexican Family Keeps Pushing to Live and Work in Leicester," *Burlington Free Press*, 16 April 1986, p. 3B.

Song

"Voices in the Hills"

by Dick McCormack*

Refrain: These mountains know more than they tell
         Yes and more than you or I ever will
         and there's magic hiding underneath the country windowsill
         And there's voices in the hills

Well my name is Gary Bartley
I was born here in these mountains
I've worked all of my adult life in the mill
My people have been farming here for seven generations
And now my brother Wayne's the only one who's farming still
The oldest tombstones in the graveyard stand over my forebears
There are hills and roads and creeks around that bear my family's name
But now like exiles in our own land
We live haunted by the old ways
Like the Indians who were driven out when first my people came
But . . . (refrain)

The old ways had their hardships and winters were too lonely
But they knew 'ere they belonged in a world they could understand
Then as the cities closed in on us
Our one choice seemed too simple
You go broke from paying taxes or get rich from selling land
But . . . (refrain)

Now my children will grow up like children of the city
Though they're living in the country, they're not living on the land
And their pleasures come in packages of Styrofoam and fiberglass
Using as a mantlepiece the tools once made by hand
And now the children of the city they come looking for the good life
Of a picture card New England, of a long forgotten day
And me I know the dream they're looking for
Believe me no one loves it more than he who held it in his hand
And watched it fade away.
But . . . (refrain)

Oh, my name is Gary Bartley
I was born here in the mountains
I've worked all of my adult life in the mill
My people have been farming here for seven generations
And now my brother Wayne's the only one who's farming still
My people have been farming here for seven generations
And now my brother Wayne's the only one who's farming still
And there's voices in the hills.

*From an album of the same name produced by Rooster Records, Bethel, Vermont, © Dick McCormack, 1976. Reprinted with permission.

Activity

Voices in the Hills
(1, 17, 18, 19)

"Voices in the Hills" is a song written by Vermonter Dick McCormack. Read his song, or listen to it if you have the record. Then answer these questions:

1. Give some reasons why Gary's brother, Wayne, is the only family member still farming.
2. How do you think Gary feels about this?
3. Why do these Vermonters, who have lived here for seven generations, feel like "exiles in their own land"?
4. Why does Gary compare their lives to the Indians'?
5. Why do you think the farmers minded getting "rich from selling land"?
6. What is the "good life" that the "children of the city" are looking for and that Gary watched fade away?
7. What are the "voices in the hills"? What do you think they're saying?
8. Do you agree with Gary's point of view? Explain.
9. Illustrate the part of the poem you like best.

UNIT 11

Government

Although we have saved the discussion of government for last, you already know many things about how Vermonters govern themselves. For instance, you know that our state constitution was written in 1777 and provided for many freedoms other states did not have. You know that town charters provided for town meetings to run the affairs of the towns. You also know that as our state grew, the responsibilities of state government grew along with it.

Vermont is a small place where every eligible citizen has the right and the opportunity to voice his or her opinion. Town meetings are the most direct route to voicing one's opinions. We are small enough so that citizens can visit the capital of Montpelier without too much traveling. We can visit with and get to know the people who represent us. To many, Vermont is "one of the last truly governable places left in America."*

Today, the two major political parties in Vermont have been alternating the governorship since the 1960s. A number of candidates from smaller parties also win offices from time to time at the local level. But it was not always so. There was a time when there were no parties. There also was a period of one hundred years when only one party controlled the State House in Montpelier. Let's go back into history to see how we became what we are today.

The Rise of Political Parties

When the state of Vermont was first established, the country had no political parties. In fact, our first president, George Washington, thought that parties might destroy the country's unity. But because people in a democracy are free to argue and voice differing opinions, our country soon divided into two parties: the Federalists and the Jeffersonians. The Federalists were followers of Washington and John Adams (our second president), who wanted a strong federal government and generally backed business interests. The Jeffersonians were followers of Thomas Jefferson, who became our third president. They were concerned that a strong federal government might squash individual rights and generally backed agrarian interests. (The Jeffersonians later split into the National Republicans and the Democrats.) In Vermont, the east-siders tended to be Federalists and the west-siders Jeffersonians.

Note

"Agrarian" means having to do with agriculture.

One Jeffersonian who fought hard for the rights of the individual was Matthew Lyon. He came to this country as a redemptioner from Ireland and settled in Connecticut. Later he moved to the Grants, was a member of the Green Mountain Boys, and founded the town of Fair Haven. Twice he was elected to the Vermont general assembly

*Frank Bryan, "Preserving Vermont's Political Heritage: Cosmetics or Culture?" in *Teaching Vermont's Heritage* (Burlington, Vermont: University of Vermont: 1984), p. 145.

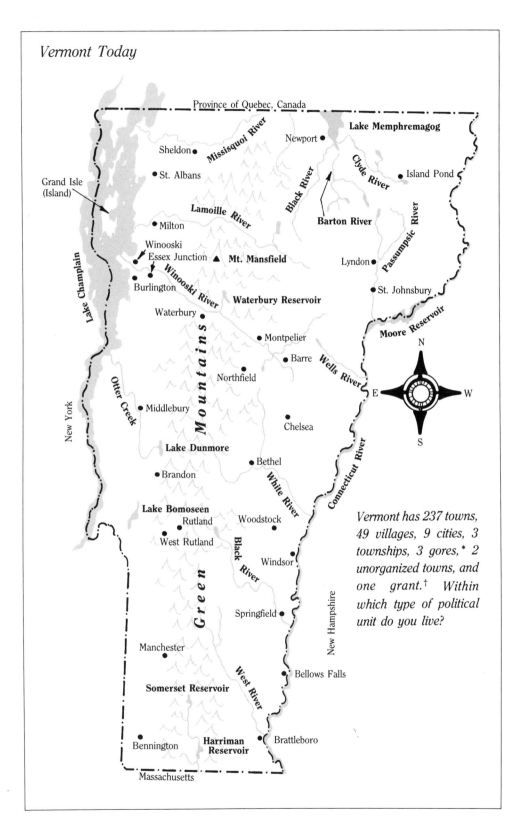

Vermont Today

Province of Quebec, Canada

Lake Memphremagog

Newport

Sheldon

Missisquoi River

Island Pond

St. Albans

Clyde River

Grand Isle
(Island)

Black River

Lamoille River

Barton River

Passumpsic River

Milton

Lyndon

Winooski
Essex Junction ▲ Mt. Mansfield

St. Johnsbury

Burlington

Winooski River

Lake Champlain

Waterbury Reservoir

Waterbury

Moore Reservoir

Montpelier

N

Barre

Wells River

Northfield

E ✦ W

Otter Creek

New York

Middlebury

S

Chelsea

Lake Dunmore

Connecticut River

Bethel

Brandon

White River

Vermont has 237 towns,
49 villages, 9 cities, 3
townships, 3 gores,* 2
unorganized towns, and
one grant.† Within
which type of political
unit do you live?

Lake Bomoseen

Rutland

Woodstock

West Rutland

Black River

Windsor

New Hampshire

Springfield

Green Mountains

Manchester

Somerset Reservoir

West River

Bellows Falls

Bennington

Harriman Reservoir

Brattleboro

Massachusetts

*A gore is land left over after towns were incorrectly surveyed.

†Warner's Grant was given to Hester Warner, widow of Seth (hero of the Battle of Bennington). It is virtually untouched to this day.

in Montpelier. Vermonters later sent him to represent them in the U.S. House of Representatives. There he gained a reputation as a quick-tempered Jeffersonian who protected the common people and their rights. He engaged in many arguments with Federalists, whom he regarded as protectors of the aristocracy.

Lyon voiced his Jeffersonian views in Congress and in his Vermont newspaper, *The Scourge of Aristocracy*, no matter what the danger to himself. In 1798, Congress passed a law called the Alien and Sedition Acts. These acts restricted the rights of people who were not citizens and made it illegal for anyone to speak out against the government (which happened to be led by a Federalist). Matthew Lyon was the first person arrested in the United States for breaking this law.

Lyon had published an editorial in his newspaper saying he would continue to speak out against the Federalist government. In October, he was arrested, tried, and convicted of sedition. He was fined one thousand dollars and sentenced to four months in an unheated Vergennes jail. You can imagine how he suffered there during the coldest months of the year.

One thing helped to ease his suffering, however. While in jail, he ran for reelection to Congress and won. Upon his release, he returned to Congress in time to cast the deciding vote for Thomas Jefferson in 1800.* The Jeffersonians were finally in power.

The Federalists gradually lost support, and the Whigs (first called the National Republicans) emerged to replace them. By the 1850s, however, the Whigs had lost support because they did not fight strongly enough against slavery. In 1854, Vermonters organized a branch of a new party, called the Republicans, to make sure slavery did not spread. They were the second state in the country to do so. You already know that most Vermonters fervently supported freeing the slaves, so it should come as no surprise that most Vermonters joined the Republican party.

Republicanism in Vermont

For the next 109 years, the Republicans ruled Vermont. Since the mid-1800s, however, there was an informal understanding among Republicans that kept the governorship bouncing from one side of the Green Mountains to the other. This became known as the "Mountain Rule." (See the list of governors in Table 11-1.) The leaders in business often were those in the governor's seat, as they had the money to run a campaign. Look over Table 11-1 and see whether you can find any familiar names.

Why did the Republicans stay in power for so long? Tradition is part of the answer. Once the farmers in the countryside settled into that party, they stuck with it. Newcomers moving to the cities were more likely to be Democrats, with the exception of the French Canadian immigrants. But because of the way the Vermont legislature was set up, city folks had a hard time winning the power game.

Since 1836, Vermont has been governed by two chambers in Montpelier: the house of representatives and the senate.† The senate had at least one representative from each county. Those counties with higher populations were allowed more. The house,

---

*None of the candidates had received a majority of the electoral votes, so the House had to choose a winner. Vermont was the last state called in the roll call.

†Prior to 1836, Vermont had only one general assembly. In that year, a thirty-member senate was established.

Governor George D. Aiken (right) declares the first Wildlife Week in 1938, as Arthur Hawkins, president of the Vermont Wildlife Federation, looks on. Aiken was governor from 1937 to 1941 and then represented Vermont in the U.S. Senate until 1975. When he retired at age 82, he was one of the most respected men in the Senate. (Courtesy Vermont Historical Society)

however, had one representative from each town or city. A city of eighteen thousand had one representative, and a town of forty-eight had one representative.

This created a house with 246 members. The towns (traditionally Republican) always outnumbered the cities. Since both chambers had to pass a bill for it to become a law, a law of urban importance would not pass unless the towns also supported it. If you wanted to get anything done, it was better to be a Republican in Vermont.

In the 1960s, Vermont's one-party rule started to crack. As you learned earlier, the population again climbed as newcomers began flowing into the state. Many of these people moved to the country, changing the character of the towns.

Even more important than this population surge were new laws. In the early 1960s, decisions in both the Vermont and U.S. supreme courts said that Vermont's one town, one representative system was unconstitutional, since every voter was not represented equally. Vermont was forced to change the rules, and since 1965 the representation in the house has been according to population. This means that the cities and larger towns now have more representatives than places of smaller populations. Vermont's house now closely reflects the one person, one vote rule. The people in Vermont's cities finally have equal representation, and urban ideas now carry more weight in Montpelier.

If you look at the list of governors, you will notice that the "Mountain Rule" no longer seems to exist today. Instead, the Democrats and Republicans have traded the governorship since the mid-1960s. Vermont's first Democratic governor in more than one hundred years was Philip Hoff, who took office in 1963. His election created a great deal of excitement for Democrats, and Vermont once again had two active parties.

In 1978, Vermonters voted Democrat Madeleine Kunin as the state's second woman lieutenant governor. (Our first had been Consuelo Northrup Bailey in 1955, the first

	Party	Yrs. in Office
Thomas Chittenden	none	1778–1789
Moses Robinson	none	1789–1790
Thomas Chittenden[2]	none	1790–1797
Paul Brigham[3]	none	1797
Isaac Tichenor	F	1797–1807
Israel Smith	J	1807–1808
Isaac Tichenor	F	1808–1809
Jonas Galusha	J	1809–1813
Martin Chittenden	F	1813–1815
Jonas Galusha	J	1815–1820
Richard Skinner	J	1820–1823
Cornelius P. Van Ness	J	1823–1826
Ezra Butler	J	1826–1828
Samuel C. Crafts	NR	1828–1831
William A. Palmer	A-M	1831–1835
Silas H. Jenison[4]	W	1835–1836
Silas H. Jenison	W	1836–1841
Charles Paine	W	1841–1843
John Mattocks	W	1843–1844
William Slade	W	1844–1846
Horace Eaton	W	1846–1848
Carlos Coolidge	W	1848–1850
Charles K. Williams	W	1850–1852
Erastus Fairbanks	W	1852–1853
John S. Robinson	D	1853–1854
Stephen Royce	R	1854–1856
Ryland Fletcher	R	1856–1858
Hiland Hall	R	1858–1860
Erastus Fairbanks	R	1860–1861
Frederick Holbrook	R	1861–1863
J. Gregory Smith	R	1863–1865
Paul Dillingham	R	1865–1867
John B. Page	R	1867–1869
Peter T. Washburn[5]	R	1869–1870
George W. Hendee[6]	R	1870

Table 11-1 Vermont's Governors[1]

J	= Jeffersonian	A-M	= Anti-Mason
F	= Federalist	W	= Whig
D	= Democrat	R	= Republican
NR	= National Republican		

[1]The governor's term was for one year from 1778 to 1870 and has been two years from 1870 to present. Until after 1912, general elections were held in September, and governors were inaugurated in October. After 1912, governors were elected in November and inaugurated in January.
[2]Died Aug. 24, 1797.
[3]Lieutenant governor; acting governor on the death of Governor Chittenden. Served Aug. 25 to Oct. 16, 1797.
[4]Lieutenant governor; governor by reason of no candidate gaining a majority.
[5]Died in office, Feb. 7, 1870.
[6]Lieutenant governor; governor by reason of the death of Governor Washburn.

	Party	Mountain Side	Yrs. in Office
John W. Stewart	R	W	1870–1872
Julius Converse	R	E	1872–1874
Asahel Peck	R	W	1874–1876
Horace Fairbanks	R	E	1876–1878
Redfield Proctor	R	W	1878–1880
Roswell Farnham	R	E	1880–1882
John L. Barstow	R	W	1882–1884
Samuel E. Pingree	R	E	1884–1886
Ebenezer J. Ormsbee	R	W	1886–1888
William P. Dillingham	R	E	1888–1890
Carroll S. Page	R	W	1890–1892
Levi K. Fuller	R	E	1892–1894
Urban A. Woodbury	R	W	1894–1896
Josiah Grout	R	E	1896–1898
Edward C. Smith	R	W	1898–1900
William W. Stickney	R	E	1900–1902
John G. McCullough	R	W	1902–1904
Charles J. Bell	R	E	1904–1906
Fletcher D. Proctor	R	W	1906–1908
George H. Prouty	R	E	1908–1910
John A. Mead	R	W	1910–1912
Allen M. Fletcher	R	E	1912–1915
Charles W. Gates	R	W	1915–1917
Horace F. Graham	R	E	1917–1919
Percival W. Clement	R	W	1919–1921
James Hartness	R	E	1921–1923
Redfield Proctor	R	W	1923–1925
Franklin S. Billings	R	E	1925–1927
John F. Weeks	R	W	1927–1931
Stanley C. Wilson	R	E	1931–1935
Charles M. Smith	R	W	1935–1937
George D. Aiken	R	E	1937–1941
William H. Wills	R	W	1941–1945
Mortimer R. Proctor	R	W	1945–1947
Ernest W. Gibson[7]	R	E	1947–1950
Harold J. Arthur[8]	R	W	1950–1951
Lee E. Emerson	R	E	1951–1955
Joseph B. Johnson	R	E	1955–1959
Robert T. Stafford	R	W	1959–1961
F. Ray Keyser, Jr.	R	E	1961–1963
Philip H. Hoff	D	W	1963–1969
Deane C. Davis	R	E	1969–1973
Thomas P. Salmon	D	E	1973–1977
Richard A. Snelling	R	W	1977–1985
Madeleine Kunin	D	W	1985–

[7]Resigned and appointed U.S. district judge by President Truman, Jan. 16, 1950.
[8]Became governor when Governor Gibson resigned, Jan. 15, 1950.

Information from: Samuel Hand and Nicholas Muller, *In a State of Nature: Readings in Vermont History* (Montpelier, Vermont: Vermont Historical Society, 1982).

woman elected to that office in our nation.) In 1985, Kunin became Vermont's first woman governor. It had taken sixty-four years since the Nineteenth Amendment was passed to elect a woman to that office. Old traditions die hard sometimes.

Vermont Government Today

One of the purest forms of democracy is the town meeting. This New England tradition has taken place in Vermont since the earliest English settlers arrived in the 1700s. Today, the first Tuesday in March is "Town Meeting Day." Any citizen is allowed to voice his or her opinion at these meetings and vote on town matters.

In recent years, many town meetings have included issues that are of interest to the world at large, such as a nuclear arms freeze and U.S. foreign policy. Some Vermonters believe that the town meeting is a good place to discuss these matters because it is the one place where every citizen has a voice. Others believe that only

The Boston Globe *depicted Philip Hoff as a reincarnated saint in this 1962 political cartoon. Hoff was the first Democrat elected governor in Vermont in modern times. (Courtesy of* The Boston Globe*)*

local issues should be discussed at town meetings, as other forums for discussion of national and international items exist. What do you think?

According to our state constitution, Vermont has three branches of government. The *executive branch* is composed of a lieutenant governor and governor elected every two years. This branch manages all the government agencies and proposes a budget to the legislature to run the state. The governor often represents the state in Washington, D.C., when it needs to negotiate with the federal government. (S)he must make many difficult leadership decisions that affect the state.

You have already read about some of these leadership decisions, from Martin Chittenden's protesting the War of 1812 to Deane Davis's pushing for Act 250. In 1985, Governor Kunin took a strong stand on another issue of great importance to Vermonters. The U.S. Department of Energy was searching for a place to bury radioactive waste products from nuclear power reactors. Nine spots in our state were being considered.

Governor Kunin opposed the plan. She wrote many letters and talked to other governors. She believed that the whole plan was dangerous, including both transporting these hazardous wastes long distances and burying them in the ground. (The wastes remain radioactive for thousands of years; no container lasts that long.) Citizens also spoke out at public hearings throughout the state. Vermonters made their outrage known. Republicans and Democrats, businesspeople and farmers all said, "No, we will resist. You will not put a nuclear waste dump in our Green Mountains."

In January 1986, the Department of Energy announced a shortened list for consideration. Not one Vermont site was on the list. People credited the leadership of the governor and Vermont's outspoken citizens for this decision. One man from Wolcott praised the fact that the "life-giving spirit of resistance and self-determination still exists" in Vermont. He was "grateful to be a part of this place and its future."* Many of Vermont's citizens feel the same way.

Another branch of government is the *legislative branch.* This is composed of the house of representatives and the senate. The representatives in these two chambers make the laws for the state. The senate has thirty members and is presided over by the lieutenant governor. The house has one hundred fifty members and chooses a speaker to run its sessions. The lawmakers meet from January to sometime in the spring. They write bills, argue the bills' pros and cons, and pass some of them into laws. Both chambers must pass a bill before it becomes a law (see Chart 11-1).

People called lobbyists work for organizations around the state and try to influence the legislators' decisions. They bring facts and figures to the lawmakers that support the points of view of their organizations. Since our legislators do not have large staffs and do not have time to research all the bills, they generally welcome discussions with lobbyists. Some groups that hire lobbyists are ski areas, the Vermont Chamber of Commerce, the Vermont Natural Resources Council, and the Coalition of the Handicapped. It is also important for citizens to lobby the legislature unofficially by writing letters, telephoning, and meeting with their representatives.

Madeleine Kunin and her family emigrated from Switzerland during World War II to escape the Nazis. In the 1984 election, she became the first woman governor of Vermont. For the first time in history, the Democrats also gained control of the Vermont senate. (Courtesy of Gillian Randall, FOTO SHOP)

Many issues discussed in Montpelier each year have historical roots. One bill passed in 1986 has a history that goes back millions of years: The senate passed a bill that would protect Champ, the Lake Champlain monster. (The house had passed it in 1982.) The 1986 legislature also passed laws to protect the state's wetlands and set new standards for water quality. Farmers got a boost from a new tax law. No longer will they automatically have to pay high taxes on their land based on how much it might be worth if they sold it to developers. From now on they may be taxed at a lower farmland rate. Another bill will help out-of-work people find jobs by attracting industry to areas of high unemployment. As you can see, the environment, farms, and jobs still continue to be of great concern to Vermonters.

The third branch of government is the *judicial branch.* This is composed of the state's courts. Citizens have a right to a trial by jury if they are charged with breaking a law. Judges preside over courts in each municipality and county. If a citizen feels

*David Budbill, "Nuclear Waste: A Community Issue," *Vermont Life,* Winter 1985, p. 13.

Chart 11-1

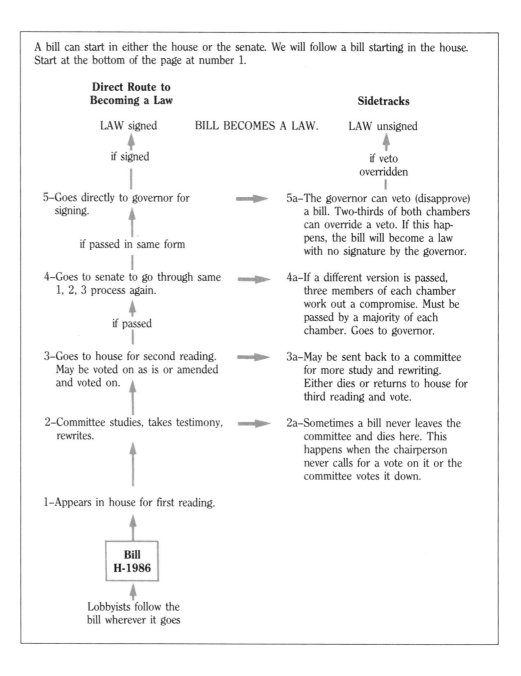

A bill can start in either the house or the senate. We will follow a bill starting in the house. Start at the bottom of the page at number 1.

**Direct Route to
Becoming a Law**   **Sidetracks**

LAW signed   BILL BECOMES A LAW.   LAW unsigned

↑   ↑
if signed   if veto
overridden

5–Goes directly to governor for   →   5a–The governor can veto (disapprove)
signing.   a bill. Two-thirds of both chambers
can override a veto. If this hap-
if passed in same form   pens, the bill will become a law
with no signature by the governor.

4–Goes to senate to go through same   →   4a–If a different version is passed,
1, 2, 3 process again.   three members of each chamber
work out a compromise. Must be
if passed   passed by a majority of each
chamber. Goes to governor.

3–Goes to house for second reading.   →   3a–May be sent back to a committee
May be voted on as is or amended   for more study and rewriting.
and voted on.   Either dies or returns to house for
third reading and vote.

2–Committee studies, takes testimony, →   2a–Sometimes a bill never leaves the
rewrites.   committee and dies here. This
happens when the chairperson
never calls for a vote on it or the
committee votes it down.

1–Appears in house for first reading.

↑

**Bill
H-1986**

↑

Lobbyists follow the
bill wherever it goes

(s)he has not been treated fairly in those courts, (s)he may appeal to the Vermont supreme court.

One issue with which the courts recently have had to deal is the ancient rights of the Abenaki. As we discussed in Unit 1, the Abenaki "disappeared" into Vermont's backwoods and wetlands for more than a hundred years. During the 1960s, however, many changes made it necessary for Vermont's Native Americans to reassert their rights. Hunting and fishing regulations were becoming stricter, interfering with the Abenaki's traditional way of life. The establishment of the Missisquoi Wildlife Refuge in Swanton made it illegal for them to hunt and fish on their traditional lands.* The Abenaki decided

*The highest number of Native Americans live in Franklin County.

to reorganize to preserve their way of life. Proudly, they came forward to protest government restrictions and fight for their ancient rights as Vermont's original inhabitants.

As a first step, they asked for formal recognition as the Abenaki nation from the governor, Thomas Salmon. He granted it in 1976. The next year, the new governor, Richard Snelling, took away that recognition. He believed the Native Americans should not have any special recognition.

Next they petitioned the state to restore their traditional hunting and fishing rights. Since it is their way of life—not a sport—they felt that they should be exempt from seasonal regulations, size limits, and licensing. They would monitor themselves according to their traditional rules. Their petition was denied.

Finally, they decided to try the judicial branch of government. During the spring of 1978, a group of Abenaki held a "fish-in" on the banks of the Missisquoi River. Thirty-four people fished without licenses, hoping to be arrested and taken to court. There they would argue their case, and perhaps the courts would restore their rights. Legal action was taken, but the Vermont district court dropped the charges in 1983. That same year, they held a second fish-in to try to force the courts to hear them. As of 1986, their case was still pending in the Vermont supreme court.

No one knows what the outcome of the Abenaki's fight will be. But like many Vermonters, past and present, they are standing up and demanding to be heard. If they had given up and disappeared "as a people, just because their continued presence (was) inconvenient or upsetting to some, all of humanity (would be) in trouble. The Abenakis have not given up and disappeared, and we can all take encouragement from that fact."*

From Today to Tomorrow

We end with the Abenaki because they were Vermont's first people. They have been here longer than any other group, treading the valleys and peaks of the Green Mountains. Thousands of years of history have been played out before their eyes. What does the future hold for them?

What does the future hold for any of us? Our past holds many clues—it is the lens through which we can view the things to come. One fact the past teaches us is that change is inevitable. No one has ever been able to stop it. We can affect only the direction of change through our actions or inaction.

The past tells us we are a part of the ecology of our earth no less than the plants and animals. We use and depend on every part of our environment. Our carelessness in the past has taught us this. We now know it is our job to treat our surroundings with respect and protect them from damage.

The past also tells us that our lives are linked to each other. What we do affects our neighbors and vice versa. We must care about what happens to them. Vermonters have always realized this and often have worked together to solve common problems. In addition, they often have lent a helping hand to others in need.

Our past shows that most people in our state have links to another place in the world through their ancestors who immigrated here. Whether they came three hun-

*William Haviland and Marjory Power, *The Original Vermonters* (Hanover, N.H.: University Press of New England, 1981), p. 263.

dred years ago or three years ago, the situation is the same. The cultural patchwork created by newcomers may bring problems and may appear to rip at the seams from time to time. But it also enriches our lives with a wonderful pattern of colors and ideas. We must learn to understand and respect the diverse customs in our state.

Our past makes us aware of a life-giving resistance, which has always been alive in our mountains and valleys. Vermonters are thinking people who decide for themselves the right or wrong of a situation and speak out against any perceived wrong. They realize that it is their duty to take an active role in the affairs of their state. Vermont is small enough that any voice can be heard, and the voices of Vermonters have never been stilled when they see a wrong that needs righting.

As long as we learn from our past and carry on in our best Vermont traditions, we can solve any problem that the future holds. We can adapt creatively to any changes. Our past tells us that the future is up to us. What will we make of it? What will *you* make of it?

Activity

Getting a Bill Passed in Vermont
(1, 2, 3, 4, 5, 8, 9, 10, 14, 18, 19, 20)

Making a bill into a law is a complicated process, as the chart on page 116 shows. Reread the chart, then follow the directions given here. When you are finished, you will *really* understand the process.

1. Write a bill you believe should become a law. You may be interested in an issue you studied in this section on the twentieth century, or you may think that another issue is important.
2. As a class, choose two (or more) of the bills you would like to see become laws. One bill will start in the house, the other in the senate.
3. Your teacher will divide the class into house members, senators, and lobbyists. The class will vote on a lieutenant governor to preside over the senate. House members must choose a speaker to preside over them. Lobbyists must decide to be for or against the bills. Your teacher will be the governor.
4. When all the roles are settled, each chamber will proceed through each step in the bill chart. The speaker of the house and the lieutenant governor will keep things running smoothly with the help of the governor. They will assign people to committees and generally keep order.
5. Lobbyists and committee members may have to go to the library or consult with experts from time to time. This could take place during school hours or be given as homework.
6. The exercise is over when the bills either die in committee, are voted down, or become laws. Have bill-signing ceremonies for those that pass both chambers. Have a revote on those the governor vetoes.

    If you pass a bill that you think is very special, send it to a representative from your county. Ask him or her to sponsor it in the next session of the legislature.

Appendixes

APPENDIX A   # Reasoning Competencies

1. The pupil can observe and report data from an experience.
2. The pupil can identify the problem or issue presented in an experience.
3. The pupil can suggest possible causes of a problem.
4. The pupil can suggest some solutions to a problem.
5. The pupil can predict consequences of problem solutions.
6. The pupil can identify similarities and differences between items.
7. The pupil can put items into groups as described by others.
8. The pupil can put items into his or her own groups and explain the criteria used.
9. The pupil can put things into serial order.
10. The pupil can distinguish between statements of fact and statements of opinion.
11. Given a dilemma situation, the pupil can take at least two positions and give reasons for each.
12. From a chart, graph, table, map, or list of facts, the pupil can state a summary or conclusion based on the data.
13. From a list of data and several possible conclusions, the pupil can identify those conclusions that could be validly drawn from the data.
14. The pupil can gather data on a given topic from at least three different sources.
15. The pupil can select and organize data on a given topic into a meaningful report.
16. The pupil can elaborate on, or give many answers to, a question.
17. The pupil can analyze information—that is, separate it into its parts.
18. The pupil can think creatively—that is, put information together in an original way.
19. The pupil can evaluate information—that is, judge it according to his or her own standards.
20. The pupil can apply knowledge to action situations.

Numbers 1 to 15 are state requirements for reasoning skills. Numbers 16 to 20 have been added by the author.

APPENDIX B

Writing Plays

1. Setting: The exact place and time should be decided first. For early efforts, try not to change scenes. With more experience, you might change scenes once or twice.

2. Characters: Make a list of characters. Make sure there are plenty of parts for the whole class. A crowd scene is helpful.

As you write, watch out for stereotyping. Male and female stereotypes often found in books and in the media involve active, intelligent, confident, and brave men and inactive, unintelligent, unsure women who need men to solve their problems. Be careful about having your characters fall into these categories. Make them more realistic.

3. Plot: Decide on the plot (or plan of action) before you start writing. The beginning will introduce the characters and the main conflict of the play. The middle will be the excitement: how the characters attempt to solve the conflicts. The last part is an interesting ending that pulls all the loose ends together. Write an outline before you begin.

4. Form: Look at a sample of a play so you can write it in the correct form. Start with a list of characters. Describe the setting (time and place). Do not use quotation marks. Put stage directions in parentheses. Use a narrator to move the action along when it is not possible to do it using conversation.

5. Decision-making: Try to make most of your own decisions concerning the writing, costuming, and scenery. Ask an adult only when you are really stuck; you may lose a valuable opportunity to make mistakes and learn from them. You are not a professional (yet), so do not worry about doing a professional job. Perform your plays only in the classroom until the quality improves enough for an audience.

6. Practicing: Spend the beginning sessions on characterizations. In other words, decide how the characters would feel and act in given situations. Try to understand the characters.

Practice only a few times with the script until you have the main feelings and ideas of the plot. Improvise when you do not remember a line. It will sound more natural, and you will be less nervous about making mistakes.

Another option: After discussing the setting, characters, and plot, you could improvise the play without using a script.

Note

A stereotype is a fixed image of a whole group of people. It is not true to life since people are too diverse to fit into a single image.

Note

"To improvise" means to make up something on the spur of the moment.

APPENDIX C   # Written Assignments

Writing is an important skill that helps you listen to your own thoughts; reinforces understanding of concepts by organizing your thoughts on paper; and helps you understand society. Therefore, writing is very important if you do not want to lose touch with yourself and your surroundings.

Below are eight criteria for evaluating written assignments. The first five can be your responsibility. Form small editorial groups that meet after each assignment and proofread each other's papers. It is a nice way of sharing your work and easing some of the correcting load on your teacher. Your teacher will look over your work to check organization, language, and sentence patterns.

Criteria for Evaluating Written Assignments

1. *Proofreading*—carefully read over the papers in your group.
2. *Punctuation*—check for periods, commas, quotation marks, and so on.
3. *Capitalization*—make sure all proper nouns and beginnings of sentences are capitalized.
4. *Neatness*—make sure the writing is legible and papers are neat.
5. *Spelling*—have a dictionary to check spelling.

Writing in a particular subject area:

6. *Organization*—use a topic sentence, limited subject matter, and logical sequence.
7. *Language*—use the subject matter vocabulary correctly.
8. *Sentence pattern*—use various types of sentences: simple, compound, and complex.

Creative writing:

6. Introduce characters and setting first. Have a logical plot, or plan of action.
7. Use concrete, descriptive language to help the reader "see" the action.
8. Include dialogue, written the way the character would speak. Use various types of sentences.

APPENDIX D   # Oral Histories

Oral histories give you an opportunity to participate actively in the process of learning. You will learn not only history but also interviewing and social skills; reading, writing, and speaking skills; and an appreciation of the lives of others. You also may learn that learning can be fascinating—a fact that will enrich the rest of your life.

Elliot Wigginton, who started an oral history project called Foxfire, says that "unpredictable, immensely powerful things happen to students' perceptions of themselves and their roots and their culture" when they do oral histories. "A sense of compassion and of basic human dignity in all its manifestations is a part of it. . .[and] the unshakable realization that all of us are a part of a grand continuum of life" is another part.* Not many activities can make such claims.

Following are suggestions for doing oral histories in conjunction with this book. Jump in and have fun!

1. In small groups or individually pick a topic to investigate. (The whole class may want to work together. In that case, one interviewee will be invited to come to class.) Topics may include the history of your family, local transportation, local industry, or the contributions of ethnic groups to your locality.
2. Find people who are willing to be interviewed. You can do this in person or by telephone and should practice what to say before you begin. The community has many different places to find interesting people. Your own home, the local history society, ethnic clubs, libraries, senior citizens' groups, nursing homes, and ethnic restaurants are just a few.

    Tell your contact person that you will give him or her a copy of the questions before the interview. This will give the person time to think about the past and to check facts.
3. Draw up a list of questions. What do you want to learn from the interviewee? Try to ask questions that require long answers, not just yes or no.
4. Send the questions to the contact person and set up a time and place for the interview. Practice using the tape recorder and role-play with classmates how to act at the interview. Ask your teacher for ideas on how to use positive reinforcement with the interviewee.
5. When doing the taping, make sure everyone is comfortable. The session should last about one hour. A second appointment should be made if more time is needed.
6. Ask the contact person to sign a release form.
7. Prepare a typed manuscript of the interview. Parent volunteers could help, or you could use the pause button on the recorder to transcribe the interview. Edit the transcript to prepare a report for the class. Tapes and transcripts should be placed in the library and/or local history societies for others to use.

This is a learning experience; don't be afraid of making mistakes. As you gain more experience, your interviews will be better.†

*"The Foxfire Approach: It can work for you," *Media and Methods* (November 1977), p. 52.

†Adapted from Norman C. Machart, "Doing Oral Histories in the Elementary Grades," *Social Education* (October 1979), pp. 479–480.

Selected References

Bassett, T.D. Seymour, ed. *Outsiders Inside Vermont*. Canaan, N.H.: Phoenix Publishers, 1976.

_____. "500 Miles of Trouble and Excitement: Vermont Railroad, 1848–61," *Vermont History* 49, No. 3 (Summer 1981), pp. 133–154.

Benton, R.C. *The Vermont Settlers and the New York Land Speculators*. Minneapolis: Housekeeper Press, 1894.

Blejwas, Stanislaus, and Lynda Slominski. *The Poles*. Storrs, Conn.: The University of Connecticut World Education Project, no date given.

Clifford, Deborah. "Clarina Howard Nichols, Editor and Crusader for Women's Rights," *Vermont Women*, November 1985, pp. 31–32.

Crockett, Walter Hill. *Vermont the Green Mountain State*, Vol. 1. New York: The Century History Company, Inc., 1921.

Cunningham, Rev. Patrick. "Irish Catholics in a Yankee Town: A Report About Brattleboro, Vermont, 1847–1898," *Vermont History* 44, No. 4 (Fall 1979), pp. 189–197.

Currance, Pam. *Vermont's Original Inhabitants*. Montpelier, Vermont: Vermont Historical Society, no date given.

Day, Gordon. *The Identity of the St. Francis Indians*. Ottawa, Ontario: National Museum of Canada, 1981.

Doyle, William. *The Vermont Political Tradition, and Those Who Helped Make It*. Barre, Vermont: Northlight Studio Press, 1984.

Duffy, John. *Vermont: An Illustrated History*. Northridge, Calif.: Windsor Publications, 1985.

Ellison, Walter G. *A Guide to Birdfinding in Vermont*. Woodstock, Vermont: Vermont Institute of Natural Science, 1981.

Elwert, Philip F. "All Around Robinson's Barn: A Social History of the Vermont Farm," *Vermont History News*, November/December 1985, pp. 125–139.

Fisher, Dorothy Canfield. *Vermont Traditions*. Boston: Little, Brown and Company, 1953.

Graffagnino, Kevin. *The Shaping of Vermont: From Wilderness to Centennial, 1749–1877*. Bennington, Vermont: Bennington Museum, 1983.

Hand, Samuel, et al. " 'Little Republics': The Structure of State Politics in Vermont 1854–1920," *Vermont History* 53, No. 3 (Summer 1985), pp. 141–166.

Hand, Samuel, and Nicholas Muller, eds. *In a State of Nature: Readings in Vermont History*. Montpelier, Vermont: Vermont Historical Society, 1982.

Harvey, Dorothy Mayo. "The Swedes in Vermont," *Vermont History* 28, No. 1 (January 1960), pp. 39–62.

Haviland, William, and Marjory Power. *The Original Vermonters.* Hanover, N.H.: University Press of New England, 1981.

Hill, Ralph Nading. *Lake Champlain, Key to Liberty.* Montpelier, Vermont: Vermont Life Magazine, 1976.

Jellison, Charles A. *Ethan Allen: Frontier Rebel.* Syracuse, N.Y.: Syracuse University Press, 1983.

Jones, Maldwyn. *American Immigration.* Chicago: University of Chicago Press, 1960.

Jones, Matt Bushnell. *Vermont in the Making (1750–1777).* Cambridge, Mass.: Harvard University Press, 1939.

Judd, Richard M. *The New Deal in Vermont: Its Impact and Aftermath.* New York: Garland Publishing, Inc., 1979.

Kellogg, Julia R. "Vermont's Post Roads and Canals," in *Reprints From Vermont History.* Montpelier, Vermont: Vermont Historical Society, 1975, pp. 80–94.

Klitz, Sally Innis. *The Jews.* Storrs, Conn.: The I.N. Thut World Education Center, 1980.

Lowenthal, David. "The Vermont Heritage of George Perkins Marsh." Address Before the Woodstock Historical Society. Woodstock, Vermont, 1960.

Ludlum, David M. *Social Ferment in Vermont.* New York: AMS Press, Inc., 1966.

McHenery, Stewart G. "Vermont's Sleepy Hollow: The Dutch Colonial Landscape Legacy," *Vermont History* 47, No. 4 (Fall 1979), pp. 279–285.

McKinney, Margot. *The Welsh Heritage of the Slate Belt.* Poultney, Vermont: Journal Press, 1976.

Meeks, Harold A. *Time and Change in Vermont.* Chester, Conn.: The Globe Pequot Press, 1986.

Merrill, Perry H. *Vermont Under Four Flags (1635–1975).* Montpelier, Vermont: by author, 1975.

_____. *Roosevelt's Forest Army.* Barre, Vermont: by author, 1981.

Morrissey, Charles T. *Vermont: A History.* New York: W.W. Norton and Company, 1984.

Mueller, Robert, et al. *Vermont's Untold History.* Burlington, Vermont: The Frayed Page Collective, 1976.

Muller, Nicholas, et al. *Growth and Development of Government in Vermont.* Waitsfield, Vermont: Vermont Academy of Arts and Sciences, 1970.

The Original Constitution of the State of Vermont, 1777 (a facsimile). Montpelier, Vermont: Vermont Historical Society, 1977.

Palmer, Peter S. *History of Lake Champlain (1609–1814).* Albany, N.Y.: J. Munsell Company, 1866.

Pepe, Faith Learned. *Vermont Workers, Vermont Resources.* Brattleboro, Vermont: Brattleboro Museum and Art Center, 1984.

Pettengill, Samuel B. *The Yankee Pioneers.* Rutland, Vermont, and Tokyo, Japan: Charles E. Tuttle Company, Inc., 1971.

Picher, Robert L. "The Franco Americans in Vermont," *Vermont History* 28, No. 1 (January 1960), pp. 59–62.

Pierce, Ken. *A History of the Abenaki People.* Burlington, Vermont: University of Vermont Instructional Development Center, 1977.

Samuelson, Myron. *The Story of the Jewish Community of Burlington, Vermont.* Burlington, Vermont: by author, 1976.

Siebert, Wilbur H. *Vermont's Anti-Slavery and Underground Railroad Record.* Columbus, Ohio: The Spahr and Glenn Company, 1937.

SPAN Consultants and Staff. "Six Problems for Social Studies in the 1980's," in *Social Roles: An Alternative Approach to K–12 Social Studies.* Boulder, Colorado: Social Science Education Consortium, 1982, pp. 80–90.

Stilwell, Lewis D. *Migration From Vermont.* Montpelier, Vermont: Vermont Historical Society, 1948.

Tomasi, Mari. "The Italian Story in Vermont," *Vermont History* 28, No. 1 (January 1960), pp. 73–85.

True, Marshall, et al., eds. *Teaching Vermont's Heritage.* Proceedings of the Second Working Conference on Vermont's Heritage for Teachers. Burlington, Vermont: University of Vermont, 1984.

_____. *Vermont's Heritage: A Working Conference for Teachers.* Burlington, Vermont: University of Vermont, 1983.

Wittke, Carl. *We Who Built America: The Saga of the Immigrant.* Cleveland, Ohio: Case Western Reserve University, 1967.

Woolfsen, Peter. "The Heritage and Culture of the French Vermonter: Research Needs in Social Sciences," *Vermont History* 44, No. 2 (Spring 1976), pp. 103–108.

Index

About the Author

Elise A. Guyette grew up in Rutland, Vermont, and earned a bachelor's and a master's degree in education at the University of Vermont. In addition to serving as a classroom teacher in three Vermont schools, she has conducted Resource Agent Programs throughout the state, run a summer session course at the Shelburne Museum, and written numerous articles and developed curricula dealing with Vermont history and culture. She is a member of the Vermont Historical Society and the League of Vermont Writers, and she is an advisory board member of the University of Vermont Center for World Education. She is the recipient of a national award for curriculum development. Presently, she is working in the School Services Department at the Shelburne Museum. She lives in South Burlington, Vermont, with her husband and daughter.